Able

How God showed two
physically disabled sisters what they
are able to do through Him

By Allison Werne, Gail Werne,
and Korrine Whitehead

With Laura Seger McAninch

Published by Legacy Press
Your life tells a story; we can help you write it.
www.legacypress.org

Scripture texts in this work are taken from the *New American Bible, revised edition* © 2010, 1991, 1986, 1970 Confraternity of Christian Doctrine, Washington, D.C. and are used by permission of the copyright owner. All Rights Reserved.

Printed in the United States of America

ISBN (paperback): 978-1-957026-12-1
ISBN (eBook): 978-1-957026-13-8

Available from Amazon.com and other retail outlets

Cover design and interior design and layout by Nelly Murariu at PixBeeDesign.com

*This book is dedicated to anyone who
feels even slightly defeated by their physical bodies.
God sees you, God knows you, and
God loves you immeasurably.*

CONTENTS

PART THREE: How do we let God guide our lives? 105

PART FOUR: Why do we want to help others with physical disabilities? 147

Foreword

by Bill Benner,
sports journalist & Special Olympics advocate

I was blessed to have a career in sports journalism that lasted 45 years and took me around the nation and world.

For The Indianapolis Star, I covered three Olympic Games (Barcelona, Atlanta, Seoul), two Pan American Games (Indianapolis and Havana, Cuba), more than 25 NCAA Final Fours, Masters and U.S. Open golf, NBA playoffs, and finals and many, many other notable events.

In doing so, I wrote about the exploits of many world-famous athletes: sprinter Carl Lewis, basketball stars Michael Jordan and Larry Bird, golfers Jack Nicklaus and Arnold Palmer, gymnast Mary Lou Retton, swimmers Michael Phelps and Matt Biondi, diver Greg Louganis . . . just to name a few.

Again, I was blessed.

But among all those faces and places that created headlines, one of my favorite moments in sports occurred in a swimming pool in Terre Haute, Indiana.

As background, my wife, Sherry, was an occupational therapist who worked at an Indianapolis school that worked with special needs students.

One day, she informed me that the school was hosting a Special Olympics Indiana track and field competition and they were in need of volunteers.

So I volunteered. And like so many, I was instantly hooked on what I witnessed . . . which was the essence of sports. Young athletes were competing for the sheer joy of competing. Where they finished didn't seem to matter.

That led to a long relationship with Special Olympics Indiana. I eventually joined the board of directors in 2002 and have remained on the board since, serving two years as chairman.

Fast forward to that Terre Haute swimming pool.

Each year, along with other board members, I would attend the Summer Games at Indiana State University. In addition to participating in opening ceremonies, I made it a point to go to various venues to watch the athletes compete.

This particular year, it included a visit to the campus pool to watch the swimmers.

It was there, in one of the heats, I noticed a young lady coming to the edge of the pool in a wheelchair.

She got out of the chair, put on goggles and a swim cap, and gingerly entered the pool.

I looked at the event program. Her name was Allison Werne. She was from Huntingburg, Indiana.

The starter's pistol sounded, and off they went. Allison's strokes were mighty, but labored. She was giving all she had, but it would not be enough to match her competitors.

It didn't matter.

The last shall be first.

In short order, the other swimmers finished the two laps, and climbed out of the pool, leaving Allison alone to finish. But quickly, the spectators — including me — became enraptured with the effort Allison was giving . . . stroke by stroke by stroke she was determined to finish the race.

And when she did touch the timing pad, the crowd erupted in applause and cheers for her courageous effort. As she climbed out of the pool, removed her cap and goggles and got back in her wheelchair, she smiled and raised her arms in triumph.

And thus, the motto of Special Olympics: Let me win, but if I cannot win, let me brave in the attempt.

Every time I hear that phrase, I think of Allison.

The last shall be first . . . in terms of bravery, courage, effort.

I have watched Allison swim many times since. She never ceases to give anything less than her best.

And she never fails to inspire.

Introduction

This book is a heart project with God. I want to be very clear about our intent to be authentic and true to these beautiful ladies' stories and to God, who has called us to share these stories. This is both a keepsake and a legacy that we want to share in hopes of helping others.

Ever since Allison was a young teenager, she had it on her heart to share her life in a book to explain what life is like to live with cerebral palsy. At that time, nobody foresaw that her older sister, Korrine, would also be in a wheelchair from a different physically disabling disease called multiple sclerosis. Together, they have inspired and motivated each other, so they began sharing their testimonies of living positive, fruitful lives with physical disabilities as presentations to groups. This process sparked them to consider a combined book project and they asked me, Laura, to help them. Unbeknownst to Korrine and Allison, God had laid a call upon my heart to write in serving Him nearly two years before they asked me to help them. This call from God sat on my soul for two years while I discerned things, and God finally revealed what that call was when He connected Korrine to ask me to write for them. From its conception, God's hands were on this book project.

Allison, Korrine, and their mother Gail have shared nearly three years of spiritual meetings with me as we progressed on God's timing in this journey of creating a book to help others. God brought us closer to Him but He also brought our families closer together in this slow and thoughtful process. In God's Divine way, He enacted this book's mission and purpose while it was being written — which is a very profound thing.

Through the process, events unfolded in my personal life and they serve as an example of why I believe this book's purpose was being lived out in a real situation while we wrote it. During the process, my adult brother lost the predominance of his eyesight due to a rare genetic disorder called LHON (Leber's Hereditary Optic Neuropathy). With Korrine's MS-damaged eyesight, she could empathize and support my brother in his lack of vision. In God's providence, He has bonded our families in order to build us up to Him. Korrine, Allison, and Gail have been there for my family as we dealt with this abrupt, life-altering physical disability ourselves. This book's purpose is to help anyone who feels even slightly defeated by their physical bodies.

How would any of us react if our family faced multiple physical disabilities? How would we mold, adapt, and mature in life's growth toward the greater good? Would we turn our disabilities into the good fruits God intended for our life? And, in the absence of a physical disability, how do we react to the particular struggles we face today? Are we progressing and ultimately growing in our faith moving closer to God? Or do we throw our hands up in the air with despair and become despondent?

Literally using their wheels and voices, Allison and Korrine show us that we cannot control the circumstances of life, but we can control the choices we make each day. We are human and there is constant disorder around us, but Jesus provides a higher order inside the disorder if we follow His lead. In following these ladies' testimonies you will see how Jesus provides divine-order in their earthly-dealt disorders.

Gail, Korrine, and Alli do not want you to read this book and wonder, "How did they do it?" or "How can they possibly choose being so positive in their disabilities now?" Instead, they want you to read this book and think, "How can I do it now?" and "What does a better choice look like in my own life?" "What are my God-abilities now?" We hope you choose to open your hearts to the messages in this book and be empowered in your own life to live more fruitfully.

This book is broken into four parts and includes a detailed table of contents so that even if you are not an avid reader, you can find the chapter that would most interest you. Like the ladies, please persevere to find the nuggets God wants for you within these pages. Read with the intent to see how God is present in these ladies' lives, but also ultimately realize how God is just as present in your life.

In all things, including this book, let us begin with prayer.

The Learning Christ Prayer

Teach me, my Lord, to be sweet and gentle in all the events of life; in disappointments, in the thoughtlessness of others, in the insincerity of those I trusted, in the unfaithfulness of those on whom I relied.

Let me put myself aside, to think of the happiness of others, to hide my little pains and heartaches, so that I may be the only one to suffer from them.

Teach me to profit by the suffering that comes across my path.

Let me so use it that it may mellow me, not harden nor embitter me; that it may make me broad in my forgiveness, not narrow, haughty and overbearing.

May no one be less good for having come within my influence; no one less pure, less true, less kind, less noble for having been a fellow-traveler in our journey toward Eternal Life.

As I go my rounds from one distraction to another, let me whisper from time to time, a word of love to You. May my life be lived in the supernatural, full of power for good, and strong in its purpose of sanctity.

This Learning Christ Prayer is from the Mother Love Prayer Book for Christian Wives & Mothers. It is the 1986 printing and is being used with permission from Fr. Joseph Tuscan, who currently serves as the national director of the Archconfraternity of Christian Mothers.

Sincerely in Christ,

Laura Seger McAninch

Why are we two sisters who both use wheelchairs?

CHAPTER ONE

Able to Accept Life's Events

*Naked I came forth from my mother's womb, and
naked shall I go back there. The Lord gave and the
Lord has taken away, blessed be the name of the Lord.*

† **Job 1:21**

As told by Gail (mother to Korrine, Allison, and Kate):

My life was forever changed on October 7th, 1981. Allison says we share a birthday on this date because of what happened to me.

Our drive into town the evening before October 7th was quiet. It was a typical, fall dusk for that time of year and it was a comfort to still see our neighbors harvesting out in their fields as the sun set. Arriving and pulling in at our hometown hospital, the maple and oak trees glistened with their autumn leaves. It was in many respects a regular Tuesday evening. While autumn characteristically has this peaceful presence, the events that followed my hospital visit to birth our second child was anything but normal and calm. As my husband, Terry, sometimes recollects, this felt like a nightmare event to him — a nightmare he cannot forget, even after four decades.

Once inside the entryway of the hospital, aromas immediately altered from the smells of the sweet harvest outside to that of antiseptic with the close of the sliding doors. The abrupt transition of smells triggered an instant "feelings switch" inside me. Before entering the hospital, I was collected, but once I was admitted as a patient, I felt limitations and a loss of my autonomy.

The hospital walls were always a source of comfort and stability for me. This was the same hospital where I worked full-time as a registered nurse, so I was in a familiar setting with dear people. Nothing was alarmingly awry. Terry was by my side as I was being admitted preparing for a normal cesarean delivery the following morning. The typical fall evening aided the naturalness of protocol for being admitted to the hospital the night before a cesarean delivery during that era of the 1980s.

"Back already? You must really love it here," Jenny, the evening nurse on duty, said. Jenny was trying to lighten the mood. I had worked a shift at the hospital just hours before. The pleasantries exchanged with a co-worker allowed me to forget I was the patient and not the nurse, at least for a few moments. After the papers were signed, I waddled into the wheelchair waiting for me. I was officially a patient. Being wheeled down the tiled, speckled, black and white floors of the hospital, we rounded the corner to an empty room.

Laying out the hospital gown on the rolling bed, Jenny gave me an amicable grin and sighed, "This is it for the night. If you need anything, you just have Terry come fetch me down the hall, okay. I have quite a few patients on the floor, so I will probably be leaving you alone for the most part." And just as cordially as she brought us into the room, Jenny departed through the heavy metal door, leaving Terry and I alone for the night.

"I think I'll call Mom and Dad Frick to let them know we are admitted and are in our room for the night. I'd also like to hear how Korrine is doing. She is so excited about the new baby. I hope she will sleep tonight for Mom and Dad considering how anxious she was earlier when we left her." Terry agreed with a grunt to my remarks. I knew he was probably pondering to himself about how much sleep anyone could get while in a hospital room.

Terry and I both had supportive, loving parents we could rely on to care for our eldest daughter, Korrine, who was 2.5 years old at the time. We felt a relief in knowing everything was as it should be at home. Our thoughts need only face what was in front of us, the birth and happy addition to our family.

Following the phone call home to mom and dad, I settled into the crunchy, starched hospital bed while Terry sat upright in the metal-framed chair parallel to the bed. There we sat; two people with the same hearts and goals for a happy family but with different insights and different dispositions. Men are often perhaps deemed unfeeling in nature, when they are essentially a species wired to be a pragmatic and temperate partner of balance to the female. We probably illustrate the generalized example of most married couples, which is what God intended in a partnership of balancing and supporting one another in the sacrament of marriage. Terry and I handle things differently, but we handle them together by helping one another. Looking back, I can see how our second child's birth story solidified us and our marriage in many unsaid ways.

Browsing the daily county newspaper, Terry attempted to relax me as he remarked about the headlines. The first headline he read was that Egypt's President Anwar Sadat was gunned down. With heavy sighs, I gave Terry a glance of disapproval which made him leap for the next headline.

The next article was pertaining to the local festival of our hometown, the Herbstfest. *Ahh,* I provided a twinkle in my eyes and Terry knew this was a safe story to read aloud to me, his expecting wife. Listening to the article as it discussed events, food booths, and entertainment, I relished in the thoughts of happy festivities. I realized that next year we could attend the Herbstfest as a family of four. My mind drifted off on future would-be tangents.

While Terry continued to read the paper, I couldn't remain quite so idle with thoughts of the future, so I reached for the new baby book in my overnight bag. The baby book's new, crisp edges opened wide with shimmering, slick pages, and the new-book smell still radiated off the pages. I soaked in its endless possibilities. Up to now, the book had remained empty from any of my tangible inputs. The flipside to the book being full of potential is that it also held many unknowns. The new life still safely within my womb was healthy and perfect at this very moment. Fixating on the book and what to write in it, my thoughts continued to meander to the future, as it did with the provocation of Terry's reading of the Hersbtfest article just moments before. The outlook with this child would presumably be filled with all the normal firsts — first smiles, first coos, first rolling over, first crawl, first steps, and the things all parents relish and delight in.

I was fatigued from already parenting toddler Korrine and from working full-time, so I just took a big pause. I exhaled a deep sigh with the book full of potential in my hands. All these mixed emotions and the high hopes of the future were heavy. It was taking a toll on me.

Jolting me out of my deep reflection with the blank baby book was a strong thrust to my lower rib cage. Ah, yes, it was the baby! In the precise moment I was most worried about the unknowns of the future I could feel the healthy baby letting his or her presence be known and recognized. The bond between mother and baby is identifiable in utero. This bond is between each and every one of a mother's kids and it never ceases, no matter their age.

I finally decided I could write in the new baby book when the new baby arrived. My thinking, analyzing, and admittedly my worrying, made my faith stumble a bit. My faith in God wasn't directly doubted, but I did worry with real concerns about delivery. I prayed and remained confident in God's triumph in all things. The baby book remained in the neutral, unwritten state as did my hopes and thoughts.

Strolling in and giving me a much-needed reprieve from all my thoughts was my nursing boss, Sheila. She made a quick stop to my room before leaving the hospital for the day. Sheila brought with her some amazing ginger snap cookies for me. Sheila knew the last hours when I would be permitted to eat a treat before the pre-surgery fasting started. The little things of life we do for one another are often the most impactful, fruitful, and lasting things. Ginger snap cookies from a loving person is the kind of thing that gets the win in the moment and is remembered even decades later. It is a fond memory for me still after all these years.

Darkness eventually covered the hospital for the night as Terry went home to be with Korrine. It created an uneasy and ominous environment. Eventually the night passed and the darkness engulfing the hospital was lifted with the onset of bustling pre-dawn activity. The action stemmed from the first-shift nurses arriving on the floors of the hospital. Upbeat conversations exchanged between the new groups of workers sounded along with the jingling of their keys and name tags. The morning's arrival, generating the change in the hospital's atmosphere, greeted me just as gladly. I was ready to start the process and prepare for the approaching cesarean delivery.

I heard my new floor nurse, Linda, grab the chart in the plastic bin outside our room. She breezed in through the same heavy door we saw Jenny walk out of the night before. "How was your night's stay? Did you sleep any? Hopefully Terry didn't eat in front of you this morning when he came in." Linda had a twinkle in her eye admitting to her intended good-humored jeers. She was aware of my plight ahead and of the fact I was on orders to fast overnight.

Linda continued, "How about we get started? The sooner we begin, the sooner you can hold your baby in your arms. It feels like just the other day that you told us you were expecting. The time has flown so fast. Hopefully the next couple of hours will fly by just as fast! It really is the homestretch now, and you have great hands all around you."

It was music to my ears. Focusing on the task at hand was exactly how I am wired to operate. I would mentally approach surgery just as I did any other task, with focus, grit, and determination. Together, Linda and I embarked on the arduous tasks of preparing for surgery. Terry bid his love and goodbyes and left to give us our needed privacy.

The years of skilled experience meant our steps in preparing for surgery were in sync with each other. Our silent actions entailing hospital gowns and intravenous lines were done under the calming ambiance of friendship. We both knew the next item needing to be done and the other provided it in a trusting ease. Concluding details were finished with Linda's succinct words, "It's time. You are officially prepped and ready for surgery."

Through the slightly ajar door, I could see Terry in the waiting room at the end of the hallway. He had found the fresh brewing coffee to grab a cup. I would see him again later in the day. Later would be perfect. I would see Terry, Korrine, and this new baby together when the time was right. This was my focus. I would focus on my family, which was my purpose.

I said a goodbye to the safe haven of a hospital room for the trek to the surgical halls. Situating myself upon the gurney, I took the role of patient by lying below my co-worker and now care provider, Linda. A forced, nervous grin summoned on my face, and I signaled I was ready to roll onward. Cognitively, I knew my free will was still intact and I could speak up, yet I somehow felt paralyzed. It felt like my power was lessened while now lying on a hard gurney.

While intense practice builds a confident athlete to face a competition, earned experience as a medical professional enabled me to have a poised exterior regardless of the interior turmoil I was feeling. The gurney's wheels, now puttering along the tiled hospital floors, echoed my intensifying heart thumps. I couldn't suppress the natural adrenaline pumping through my veins.

We journeyed further down the hospital halls to get to the surgical units. These same hallways I knew like the back of my hand; certainly, every crack in the floor below and every waning fluorescent ceiling light above were imbedded in my memory files. I was sinking deeper into the moving gurney. My perspectives had changed.

Veering to the right, the surgical room received us into its cold, sterile walls. The room had never been intimidating prior to this occasion.

Yet, the nerves incubating within me made my mind race undisciplined. Lurking above, the bright surgical lights hovered in a painfully blinding way. I rarely experienced this vantage point, because on a normal day the lights were at my backside aiding my job as a nurse.

Deciding to choose faith, I assured myself this was a safe place of medical practice. I wasn't on the open prairie about to give birth against insurmountable odds. No, I was in the best place possible, a place I valued and with people I loved.

I had transitioned my body to being a patient from the moment I laid physically on the gurney, but now it was my thoughts changing from the role of caregiver as a nurse to that of being the patient entering surgery. From the patient perspective now, the hospital had made a switch. The underlying theme of the hospital was always dark and serious, but the nervous eyes of my patients I had often overlooked and silenced with my own uplifting and compassionate care and attention for them. As the patient, I felt like a caged animal seeking exoneration. Any mother about to give birth seeks this exoneration, the fast forward button to speed ahead of the trial that lie ahead. Seeking them, I located images to gain some needed perspective. My faith was in motion when I located the warmth within my sights and within the surgical walls, and it was found in the busy hands and faces shining warmly above me.

Beyond those bright and alarming surgical lights were my indirect family members and co-workers. Over the years, I laughed and cried alongside these same faces. These faces were more than colleagues because we went to church and prayed together. Despite these warm countenances, my coworkers had a job to do, and I was indeed now the patient. As the patient, I had to surrender and resign the control I might have had on the other side of the gurney.

"I think October is a beautiful time to welcome a baby to your family, Gail. If this child has half your strength, he or she will be ready for this world." I smiled at the anesthesiologist trying to boost me up. He had an idyllic, gentle bedside manner to distract and calm patients. His tender nature and uplifting remarks lifted any of the lingering weights of worry from my shoulders. I knew I was in competent and caring hands.

Cesarean delivery is a process. Sitting upright with my legs dangling off the edge of the surgical table, my petite frame tried to attain a stone stillness as the anesthesiologist worked to analyze each step meticulously. Like a water balloon shifting inside a child's grasp, my protruding abdomen shifted in fluid waves in front of me. The infant in my womb was still in active motion, too. The already tight living quarters made the infant's movements forceful when tightened further by the forward arching of my spine.

No words were spoken as I bodily and emotionally melted into my friends' physical and professional competencies as the anesthetic for my cesarean was carefully administered at the proper location along my spine. They shouldered me and I finally accepted my role as the patient. It was a peaceful and holy acceptance of trusting my faith and trusting my coworkers. All my faculties were abandoned, but I held on to what remained when all was stripped away, which was faith.

Time moved in slow motion as I retracted back to the horizontal position on the surgical table. This is the position I would last remember being in from the surgery. What happened next was a defining moment — a moment no one could have prepared for nor predicted as a plausible outcome in their life. This is also the moment that altered our entire family's life forever. As it should have been enacted, the anesthesia started to take affect within my body. This would facilitate the prompt surgical delivery of the baby after the medicine was fully functioning. With a blade in hand, the surgical obstetrician was perched above me. He was ready to begin an incision after the confirming words from the anesthesiologist.

I remember distinctly being questioned, "How are you? Do you feel dizzy at all?"

Initially able to confirm aloud for myself, I responded, "I feel fine . . ." But my voice slowly descended to nothing, and I lost all consciousness.

Those were the last words I spoke before my heart stopped and life immediately tumbled out of control for me.

Becoming entirely more potent and powerful than expected, the anesthetic drug caused seizures to commence as the first sign of erroneous events. Continuing to wreak havoc on my body, the medicine paralyzed my lungs which ceased my breathing. The seizures spiraled to respiratory arrest followed by cardiac arrest. My heart stopped. My body was swiftly dying with my baby still in my womb.

My co-workers and the hospital priest, Fr. Joachim, shared many perspectives about the events that followed when my heart stopped. From their stories I want to share how our family was forever molded from this single, important birth story.

When my heart stopped, the hospital staff faced one of their own lying in front of them crashing into death. The shock of the events felt like a lit stick of dynamite landed on the gurney in place of my body. One nurse friend told me, "From heaven it must have looked like a nuclear hot spot for how hard they were all praying and working on you."

Terry was sitting in the waiting area outside the surgery room, and he remembers the chills he had from hearing Code Blue come across the intercom. He saw nurses running in the hallways and heard my name floating aloud from their voices. Terry says his heart sank further with worry when the hospital priest, Father Joachim Walsh, was rushed through the hallway to the same surgical room I was in.

Terry's mother, Lovie, was at home the morning of my scheduled caesarean delivery. Being a former employee of the hospital, Lovie received prompt notification of things going awry from the current head of surgery, Sister Florine Jochim, O.S.B. Despite knowing the familiar voice on the phone, it was alarming for Lovie to hear Sister Florine's chilling words that Lovie better come to the hospital. Stammering on the phone, Lovie probed further to find out what was the matter. Sister Florine simply beckoned, "Come."

Lovie remembered racing to the hospital, and she recalled seeing every doctor and available nurse hovering over the surgical table in the operating room where I lay. She located her son, Terry, in the waiting room. Together, they waited, powerless to do anything but pray and wait.

Professional and personal motives of the hospital staff formed a great cause to fight for life on that fateful October morning. When the seizures started on me, the surgeon dropped the blade intended to bring forth new life and instead he was thrust into the duty of preserving the life of me, his patient and friend. This was an emergency for the entire surgical staff.

Mine and the baby's lives were in grave danger with every minute passing where my body was without oxygen. With no heartbeat and no oxygen to my lungs and brain, it also meant no oxygen to the baby. This led to very intense resuscitations. Every person in the surgical room was working to correct the issues the anesthetic medicine had caused.

This became a cluster of time reflective of absolute nothingness for me. I saw nothing. I felt nothing. I only recall feeling fine until the moment it all went dark for me. In such a limbo state between life and death, it is very conceivable to imagine I had reflections of my family or even encounters with Jesus. Many people have asked me this, but this was not the case for me. While I can say I didn't have any out-of-body experience during this emergency, I can verify that I felt the hands of God in a different near-death experience I had years after this. Stay tuned for a later chapter on that event. While my body and mind weren't functioning during this delivery, I do feel my spirit and soul fought for life and for the life within my womb. I've always believed in God's ultimate will to be done in life.

Standing stationed in the corner of the surgical room was Father Joachim. He witnessed as the doctors and nurses worked to revive me, and he did his job of praying even more fervently as the circumstances intensified.

Four times the doctors defibrillated my lifeless body to no avail. Fr. Joachim said his eyes bounced from the clock to the doctors to my lifeless body lying on the table. It was very plausible for Fr. Joachim to imagine burying a young mother and a baby in the coming days in the church cemetery. He didn't want to think it. There had to be more than this as the outcome. God had to intervene. God had to work a miracle, a miracle for this parishioner, for this Werne family, for this church family, and for this hospital family, too. He kept praying for God's will to be done in this circumstance and for the mother and child to live.

Five minutes turned into ten minutes; fifteen minutes then stretched forward nearing the twenty-minute marker. Couldn't the time that felt like slow motion all morning during the surgery preparations simply stop altogether? Couldn't they be given more time to revive me while simultaneously delivering the baby? Endurance was tested in the surgical room. The doctors had to make decisions and execute an effective plan to save me first and then move to save the baby. This was the choice and avenue they directed their momentum toward.

The hospital team's crucial moment was met with Fr. Joachim's highest prayers. Twenty minutes had passed since the seizures had sent the surgery spiraling. Finally, an inter-cardiac epinephrine needle was plunged into my heart. This was supposedly the last effort to save my life — and to save my baby's life, too. It had to work. They had to save their colleague and friend. They had to save both of us.

Could this crazy event possibly be God's plan? Was God's plan to have Terry and Korrine be their own tiny family for the rest of life without me and this new baby? It simply could not be the plan, and Fr. Joachim prayed harder.

At the exact moment the epinephrine needle went into my heart, a gasp in unison by everyone sucked all the air out of the surgical room.

Silence blanketed the space . . . until, thump, thump, thump went the EKG monitor!

They had a heartbeat on me. It meant I was alive. This was the first sign of success and of viability. Next, they had to proceed as quickly as possible to deliver my baby, the second life needing saved. Fr. Joachim's prayers had appeared to be heard by God in my revival, but his prayers needed to be heard for my baby, too.

Shaking off the adrenaline that plagued him for nearly the last half hour, the surgical obstetrician composed himself and steadied his hand with the scapula to make an incision for the cesarean delivery. Locating the baby, they grabbed her and swiftly pulled her into life outside the womb. It was indeed a "her," a girl! She was a beautiful, full-term, precious gift of life from God!

All eyes were searching to see if anything was visibly wrong with my newborn. Her whimpers were a sign of life. The life was faint, but it echoed throughout the once bleak and morbid air of the surgical room. It was a pinnacle sign for the hospital staff to hear life from such a tragic scene.

My baby weighed a normal and healthy 7lb 4oz, but this resilient soul endured more than most newborns do in her quest to attain life. We named her Allison, Alli for short. It was a bit of an ode to our beloved doctor, Dr. Ellison, that Allison was so named.

Hours after the cesarean delivery, I awoke in an intensive care unit room without my newborn by my side, oblivious to the morning's events in surgery. I only remembered feeling fine and then my world went dark. The great gift, the great reward, from all the labor and toil of bearing a child is the newborn. Yet, I did not have the gift. Instead, I had the physical recovery of myself that needed to be expedited so that I could be reunited with my baby.

Immediately after surgery, Terry's mother, Lovie, asked, "What should I do to help?" So, our parents, along with Terry, combined forces and split their support between being with me in the ICU and being with Alli at the new hospital located an hour away. With Allison's Apgar scores being subpar and the onset of seizures, Allison was sent to a bigger city hospital and away from me. My family made choices in the heat of the moment to do what they had to do, what they thought was best, in the emergency situation. Terry stayed with me in the ICU. Terry's parents, Lovie and Jerome, and my mother, Frannie Frick, followed the ambulance carrying baby Allison. The norm of the time in 1981 meant Allison was accompanied by a nurse and doctor but driven by the local funeral director to get to the high-risk nursery center. Through it all, my family prayed.

The core of what happened was an accident. The medicine was at fault. It did not work correctly. My anesthetic drug had risen within my body to affect my lungs and respiration while also stopping my heart abruptly. Thanks to the team inside the surgical walls, Allison and I live. They never gave up on resuscitating life. It was a surgery to never forget, and it caused life-changing aftermath requiring extreme acceptance. It is in our deepest and greatest trials we must surrender and have acceptance. God's will and not ours is what prevails in the end. From the moment the traumatic events unfolded, I unconsciously accepted God's plan and it carried me through to accept the repercussions and blessings ever since intentionally and firmly.

When Fr. Joachim provided me with the gravity of what had transpired in surgery, gratefulness consumed my soul. To this day, I am appreciative for what we have as a family. It is a miracle that I survived the birthing event mostly unscathed. It is another miracle Alli survived. I chose to not look at anything that happened as negative. In choosing to accept what happened, I trust God was in control during the birth as much as I trust God is in control now. We can't change God's will. We must accept and go with it. I also pray for a miracle at night.

Saint Francis de Sales said, "One ounce of virtue practiced in tribulation is worth more than a thousand in a time of rest and joy." Virtue is moral goodness which is desired instinctively by all humans. I have tried to turn this event we lived through and the consequential effects into the strong virtues our family now stands on as our foundation. We try to continue seeking God no matter what happens to us. God has always provided blessings along the way for us to manage life. Look for the blessings — they are always there, but we won't find them if we don't accept what has happened to us.

Eventually we were reunited from our separate hospital stays and began life as a family of four. It was a week after Allison was born that I was released from the hospital. On October 19th Allison was finally released from the high-risk nursery. Life was semi-normal and descriptive of the typical ear infections and crying sprees with a newborn, but it was also abnormal due to the seizures Alli had with alarming regularity. As a newborn, Alli was on medicine to control her seizures, and she was under the watchful eyes of several doctors.

As time progressed, I noticed some peculiarity with Alli's physical disposition. Alli would sit in the "W" style — her knees bent under her, and her ankles and feet stretched backward at her sides in a w-shape. Young children have more flexibility in their hips, so it is not as uncomfortable as it appears and many healthy children prefer this style; however, the problem is if this w-shaped way of functioning is predominate and if the child is sitting in this manner as a means of supporting their lack of strength in their core. Alli was lacking proper muscular development in her core.

In addition to the "W" style of supporting herself, Alli was behind on her growth milestones during her first year of life, and her limbs would spastically manipulate. In my medical mind, I knew of the potential effects Alli might have suffered during the birth with a lack of oxygen to her brain. We sought a neurologist to determine what was going on with Alli.

Alli was eleven months old when Terry and I took her to a rehabilitation center to be further evaluated by a neurologist. In stark contrast to the supporting doctors we had during the birthing event, this doctor had a polar opposite demeanor. He simply looked us in the eyes and pragmatically stated Alli was a "vegetable" or a "noodle." He bluntly said Alli would not develop to function normally as a child.

As derogatory, offensive, and inaccurate as the words the neurologist used in noodle and vegetable to describe her, Alli was more formally diagnosed with spastic athetoid cerebral palsy or CP, as we will refer to in this book. Cerebral palsy is caused by damage to the brain before, during, or after birth, and it results in impaired muscle coordination as a primary disability.

Imagine being told your child is a noodle. Imagine being told they will not amount to anything more than what they are now. Does this fuel any righteous anger? A desire to not accept a label that pigeonholes your child into a life of limited expectations? Feelings of injustice deep within? To this date, I can't even recall this neurologist's name. I let any frustration and anger I had with the neurologist go then and there, because it wasn't what was of foremost importance to me. I simply accepted his opinion for what it was, but I also chose to view it as only one person's opinion. Harboring anger and resentment towards any doctor wouldn't help Alli or our family. In Ephesians 4:31-32 it explains, "All bitterness, fury, anger, shouting, and reviling must be removed from you, along with all malice. And be kind to one another, compassionate, forgiving one another as God has forgiven you in Christ."

I firmly believed God had more in store for Alli. We didn't agree with this doctor's dismal prognosis. We believed that God's will was more than this doctor's low expectations. In choosing holy acceptance of God's will, it buoyed us to other avenues of improving and progressing!

Alli endured tumultuous moments at her birth that shaped not just her physical life but the tenacity and strength of her spirit as well. Her spirit is God-molded and shining bright for all of us to behold. The scope of learning about and learning from Alli has just begun in this beautiful story. We hope to show that how and why things happen to us are not as vital to understand as the choice we make to accept them and move forward with the God abilities we have. Holy acceptance is when we relinquish the control we have over our earthly circumstances and move forward with God's holy will for our lives. I accepted the birthing event's repercussions, but I did not accept that the neurologist's opinion would align with God's plan for Alli's life. I knew God had more for Alli. I knew it in my spirit. Alli is absolutely a capable individual now who also happens to live with physical disabilities. Alli is a blessing to all who are lucky enough to know her.

We have a choice. Let's recognize the heavy things we carry daily and accept them for what they are. Let's allow our own personal vulnerabilities to be the catalysts for the positives coming next in life. Accept what we cannot change so that we can grow and thrive with what we do have.

⁇ Reflective Questions

1. Ponder, reflect, and name some defining moments over the years that have happened to you.

2. Explain how you accepted those defining moments. Within your vulnerability, have you found a holy acceptance to progress forward?

🙏 Closing Prayer

God, help me to be more like Job from the Bible. Job lost his farm, his livelihood, his health, and his family. He faced one obstacle after another, and he endured personal physical atrocities. Yet, Job prostrated himself, fell to the ground, and he chose to still worship God. He praised God amidst all of his heartbreak. No matter what calamities may happen to me, I want to find holy resignation and holy peace with you, God. I will remain confident in the triumph of God. I want to glorify you, in all that I do. Blessed be your name, God. Amen.

Let nothing disturb you,
Let nothing frighten you.
All things are passing away:
God never changes.
Amen.
† Saint Teresa of Avila

CHAPTER TWO

Able to Nurture Optimism & Hope

And I tell you, ask and you will receive;
seek and you will find; knock and the door will be
opened to you. For everyone who asks, receives;
and the one who seeks, finds; and to the one who
knocks, the door will be opened.

† **Luke 11:9-10**

As told by Korrine:

I was only three years old when my parents learned that my new baby sister, Allison, had CP. It is normal to have a somewhat limited understanding of cerebral palsy as an adult, so imagine the interpretation of what cerebral palsy means to a three-year-old. Yet, it was also a very natural part of my life to have a sister with physical disabilities. While Allison may have appeared physically different, she was never looked at as anything less than me. We grew up together. She is part of me as my sister. Therefore, my bond with Alli was in the purest form of sisterhood from the very beginning of our lives. We were bonded with pure, unconditional love.

Some would say it was a unique upbringing to have a sister who couldn't walk and talk like me, but I see it as the way that God molded me. My different family dynamics are what formed my resilience of character. It helped me grow strong and independent, and I am appreciating this foundation even more now later in my life.

James Baldwin said, "Children have never been very good at listening to what their parents tell them — but they never fail to imitate them." The character traits I witnessed from the unspoken actions of my mom are what I have tried imitating in my own life. She set the best example in all areas of life, so from early on I looked up to her and lived with the same can-do attitude as her.

While growing up, I watched as mom worked countless hours as a registered nurse. Mom also simultaneously sought the continual care and positive progression for Alli. These were very involved, very full, and very eventful years. Through choosing the betterment and the God-given potential for our family member Alli, it meant effort. Although, we don't describe these efforts as work. It was natural for us to roll up our sleeves and do whatever was necessary to help one another, regardless of what personal inputs we had. Mom and dad didn't stop in their quest to help Alli, so I didn't stop in my quest to assist them. This was, and continues to be, a quest with labors of love so it was never looked upon as work. Work ethics I now see were obtained as a long-term, very positive side effect from how my family interacted.

As I aged into my teen years, I was able to alleviate more of the tasks at home for both of my parents. I tried to emulate mom's high energy, perseverance, and work ethic. Mom's character traits I not only inherited through our shared genetics but they were also organically picked up from watching mom demonstrate them day in and day out — nature and nurture is the best way to explain what mom did for me.

These character traits are serving me later in life in ways no one could have foretold, but God knew. God knew all along the resilient, fighting, independent, hard-working spirit He wanted to mold in me. It did not occur overnight, but rather over years of rising above the norm of expectations for my age. My family transformed each other for the better; not just in building both of my sisters and I to be well-balanced, but also in building a more capable and independent Alli.

Daily, I got to witness the skill of how to think outside of myself in my home life. It's a gift, really, to go through life different than your peers. Well-balanced kids who have the capacity to look at the bigger picture of life are formed and taught these desirable skills in daily moments. I see my upbringing as a gift. Living through it at the time, I know I wasn't always receptive to obeying and learning from the demands of life, but as an adult, I can call it the gift that it was.

By the time I was a teenager, it is important to understand I was still grappling with what is important in life. When I felt most deflated, I looked to find my answers in my sister Alli's lived example. Alli encompasses all virtues any human desires in life. This is what is so beautiful for me to acknowledge. I found answers in the lived models of mom and Alli. I took the knowledge and did something about it because I was a doer who wanted to improve and not a passive follower of the crowds. How could I be complacent in life, when mom and Alli worked so hard to get the most out of their lives?

In high school, I was a bit of a social butterfly, and I enjoyed many activities. I gravitated to the sport of golf because my grandfather had taught me the game. Golf was a chance to connect with grandpa. This is the type of bond, a bond with a sport enjoyed between family members, that last a lifetime. When I was in high school, girls' golf was a fun aspect of the high school sports sector. I was excited to play on the inaugural team. This led to my eligibility to play golf at the collegiate level.

Not one to be idle, I also tried other sports like softball, I life-guarded at the school pool in the evenings, and I had the responsibility of being a mat maid for the wrestling team. The wrestling team was a family that I felt fortunate to be a part of. The coach became like another father figure for me, and I had a lot of friends on the team to support.

Supporting others in sports was what I enjoyed. While I was a very physically active teenager, I wasn't so much into playing the sports as much as I was into watching, motivating, and just participating to be a part of a team. The term team-player is who I tried to be. I was a team-player in my family, so I carried that over to being a team-player in school.

There was a pivotal turn I made during my senior year in high school. It was a wholesome and unscripted unfolding of events that changed the trajectory of my life for the better. As always, life turns and changes when we least expect it. And, on the debris of a previous heartbreaking relationship, life blossomed into something most unexpected and most amazing. I persevered and held onto hope. This is the case for me, and I am very grateful.

In March of my senior year, we had the annual, highly anticipated, and highly revered high school boys' basketball championships, known as Hoosier Hysteria in Indiana. I had an especially memorable basketball game the spring of my senior year.

Wrapping up my typical chores at home, I drove myself to a big night of high school basketball at the historic Memorial Gymnasium in town. My good friends played on our school's team, and I would use my high spirits to cheer them on just like I did for the wrestling team. Entering the packed gymnasium was numbing to the senses. Was everyone in the entire county packed into the stands, or did it just feel like it? Not one to be intimidated by the deafening noise and large crowds, I felt adrenaline kick in as I was magnetically pulled closer to the hardwood floors of the basketball court. In my extroverted style, I trotted down the hard, cement stairs of the historic gymnasium.

I was happy to be there, to be with friends, in the hysteria of high school basketball at its finest. I was even happier to see a great friend who had returned from college just to watch this high school sectional game. His name was Chris. Chris had graduated only a year prior and was attending a college nearby.

"Hey Chris, it's so good to see you. I didn't know you'd be back for this game." I had to scream over the noise of the crowd as I grabbed him for a giant bear hug. This was before the prevalence of cell phones and certainly before the internet and social media would have connected friends daily with their whereabouts.

"Yeah, this game landed in our schedule just perfectly so we could get away." Chris explained. Chris was the basketball team manager at the college he attended an hour away, so it made perfect sense for him to unexpectedly be at the game, except for the fact Chris had mentioned 'our' and 'we.'

Following his initial comments, another guy peeked around the side of Chris indicating he was with Chris. As a result, this prompted Chris to provide appropriate introductions amidst the energetic, thunderous atmosphere in the gymnasium. "Oh, hey Korrine, this is Chad — Chad Whitehead. He plays on the basketball team at college." Then glancing to his other side, he said, "And, Chad, this is Korrine Werne, a good friend of mine from back here."

"NO WAY! Chad Whitehead? Seriously! You mean, THE Pike County Chad Whitehead?" I couldn't contain my excitement as I found myself repeatedly belting his name over and over, louder each time I said it. I was baffled and laughing as I connected in my own head for why I knew him.

Yet, to Chad, my raucous affirmations clearly signified I knew him already. I remember Chad was grinning from ear to ear as he sat back in the wooden bleachers thoroughly amused and impressed. Evidently, I appeared like the president of "Chad Whitehead's Basketball Fan Club." Chad mistook my enthusiasm as a compliment.

Chris interjected, "So, then you know him already, Korrine?"

Painfully aware of how my next comment would sound, I tried to lessen the blow by lowering and calming my voice. "Well, my best friend and I would sit in the bleachers years ago during middle school games and ... and ... well, we watched you." I took a long pause, creating some expectancy on how the rest of my story would unfold.

We locked eyes before I continued onward in a more sobering manner. "Because we used to call you zit-face."

Here we sat, many school years later, locking eyes in the flesh, and ultimately turning red in the face over embarrassment from misperceptions of one another. You cannot say the foundation of our relationship wasn't built on honesty! And the last laugh is for Chad because my last name is Whitehead now, after all. So, all kidding aside, he won me over rather quickly after I blatantly teased him at our official introductory meeting.

Whether my high school basketball team won that night in sectional isn't as important as knowing this game laid the groundwork for me to meet my to-be partner and best friend in life. Over the hysteria of the sport of basketball on the Indiana hardwoods, we met. How eerily life foreshadows what is to come, because in our current lives, twenty plus years later, things revolve around a lot of sporting events in our sons' lives — including those same Indiana gymnasium hardwoods.

After laughing off those initial preconceptions of each other, we started dating very soon after meeting. Our first date consisted of Chad meeting both of my sisters, Alli and Kate. He spent more time with them than me! Some young ladies might be jealous of a suitor being so enamored with their sisters upon a first date, but not me. This was a beautiful thing for me to see. Between playing rummy cards with my younger sister, Kate, and then talking with Alli to truly know her, Chad's personality shone bright with his demonstrated ease and patience. He proved so much during our first date with his sincere actions. He wasn't exuberant and excessive with words. Instead, his actions spoke louder than words. His actions spoke of true character. THE Pike County Chad Whitehead was a gem of a guy. I knew it. I saw it with my own eyes, and I admit I was smitten from that point.

Our first date and all future dates, Chad gelled seamlessly into our family with not a second thought given to Alli's CP. Alli's physical disabilities were a non-issue. He wasn't scared off nor did he act awkward around Alli. Chad genuinely wanted to understand Alli, and he was patient in his introductory attempts to hear her talk. This was an important quality that I needed to see in a possible life partner. I would not accept anyone that wouldn't accept my sister and my whole family. I also knew whomever I would end up marrying in life, whenever that would be, that they needed to be on board with Alli. I had envisioned myself taking care of Alli if anything happened to mom. Before I was legally an adult, I was fully aware of what I must have in a husband, my partner in life. Yet, I didn't know what life held in store for me, either.

I graduated high school a few months after meeting Chad in the spring of 1997 and then I went on to attend college the following fall. I took up running for personal pleasure while in my independence away from home. Running helped clear my mind. I enjoyed being active. With each passing day, I also felt more confident and happier with the relationship I was building with Chad. He attended college a couple hours away from me at that point in time. It was a feeling from the early onset of our dating that assured me he was the right one.

After one semester as a freshman college student, I transferred colleges to receive a scholarship to play golf at a different college. This change allowed me to live at home to help mom care for Alli while also being closer to Chad. It was the right move for me.

When Chad was ready to propose marriage, he evidently involved Alli more than I knew. Alli was in on Chad's secret proposal attempts. That's correct, there was more than one attempt, and she assisted him with his multiple plans.

In August of 1998, Alli was living in Canada for a five-week Ability Camp focused on Conductive Education Therapies to help her with her CP. For one of those five weeks, Chad and I took a turn staying with Alli, and this is where Chad involved Alli in his wedding proposal plans.

Alli certainly enjoyed our company in Canada with her because we took her exploring on adventures. In the evenings after Alli's training was complete for the day, we'd set out and have some fun. After Chad grasped the needed difference between kilometers per hour and miles per hour while driving, there really were few other impediments to our carefree trips. We were young and enjoying good times. Alli's wheelchair was a nonfactor in these romps. Alli was game for anything — including when we carried her up a winding castle's staircase at one point! We won't disclose how that venture ended when we were spotted by a custodial worker of the castle! We had to hustle to leave!

The most memorable excursion was a visit to Niagara Falls as a larger weekend trip. This was the trip Chad and Alli had something big up their sleeves planned. Niagara Falls is a very bustling area with people from all over the world, and thus a very exciting atmosphere. Between touristy things, we took a pause to relax in the hotel. I had left Chad and Alli in the room briefly to run back to the car for a bag. Briskly trying to clear the road on my return trip from our car, I stumbled hard and fast. I twisted my ankle very badly while also falling to the ground in the middle of the street. A Good Samaritan nearby saw me fall and he pulled me to the curb, out of the line of on-coming traffic!

When I got back up to the room, Alli and Chad were thankful I was okay from falling, but with my ankle swelling and in pain, our plans to dine at the Space Needle at Niagara Falls were scratched. Unbeknownst to me at the time, Chad's plans to propose were likewise scratched for the evening. He wanted it to be special, so he waited. He patiently waited. Good things come to those who wait. Alli continued to keep her secret with Chad.

A few short weeks later and with Canada a distant memory, we were back in Indiana and Chad had some additional special plans. If Niagara Falls couldn't work, he could still make it just as special. Aspiring for an epic and memorable proposal, he arranged for us to watch a play in Louisville, Kentucky and then take a cruise on the Ohio River aboard a special boat called The Star. Chad was excited for his plans. In the end, it was perfect but not because of his well-crafted plans.

The play in Louisville proved to not be what we expected based on the title. Becoming highly disappointed in the play, we decided to leave and find our next special item on the agenda, an evening cruise aboard The Star on the Ohio River.

The theme of things not going quite as planned carried over from the play to our cruise on The Star. It was icy cold outside, so the cruise itself felt disagreeable physically, but surely the food would be worth the unpleasant cold. Splitting the boat deck down the middle were beautiful displays of food atop long tables. Our eyes lit up with the same surprise we felt at the play. While the foods were arranged artfully and appealing to the eyes, the foods themselves, like oysters and caviar, were not appealing to our taste buds and stomachs!

We tolerated the cruise until a dock arrived where we could disembark. Ultimately, we did not eat and we simply withstood the freezing temperatures. We were together though, through every uncomfortable moment. What matters most in life is being together, regardless of surroundings, events, and experiences. This is a repeating theme for Chad and I throughout our relationship — we find the blessing of just being together through thick and thin. A hopeful and optimistic mindset allows attitudes to shine bright.

From the twice derailed evening events, we settled in for the hour drive home. Stopping along the interstate in Corydon, Indiana we grabbed some memorable McDonalds to eat. We were cold and famished. A simple meal was a further reminder of not valuing perceived fancy events and special things as much as valuing one another and the people sharing the simple meal.

Finally pulling in the driveway at my mom and dad's home, Chad resolved that he had enough of his attempts at planning the perfect proposal. He was tired of trying to orchestrate and wait for the perfect moment. Big proposal ideas at Niagara Falls and ideas of a romantic big city evening all fell flat. So, in front of the home I grew up in, Chad got down on one knee and he proposed right then and there. No more planning a perfect proposal! Of course, without hesitation I said an emphatic yes.

Beautiful memories are made holy and wholesome because of the attitudes and the love of the people in the memories. For instance, memories of an idyllic wedding proposal wouldn't have the character that Chad's marriage proposal attempt(s) do.

Chad and I were married on August 5, 2000, in St. Mary's Catholic Church in Huntingburg, Indiana. It was a memorable day filled with lots of happiness and hope for the future. A highlight of our wedding mass included Bridesmaid Alli walking down the aisle with two of Chad's groomsmen. Alli literally stood up for me in support of the marriage. My heart over-flowed with joy. Alli was also overflowing with happiness because she wrote a speech for us. In my dad's unassuming way and as the patriarch of our family, he rose and spoke Alli's words aloud at the wedding reception. Dad's passive ways of communicating were now perhaps made clearer in his welcoming Chad to the family by means of Alli's speech. It was a bridge in dad's informal but very kind manner towards Chad.

With sisters as close as Alli, Kate, and I, it might leave one to wonder if it was bitter-sweet to see the first one of us married and branching off from the family tree. This was just not the case for us. Chad joined our family and it only made us bigger, tighter, and happier. Chad and I never gave up on hope while patiently waiting for the right partner in life. Nor did Chad lose hope in his quest for a unique engagement.

Christopher Reeve was a famous actor portraying Superman in the late 1970s and 1980s. Although he played Superman, a horse-riding accident in 1995 left him in a wheelchair as a quadriplegic. Shortly after this accident he was quoted as saying, "Once you choose hope, anything's possible." Indeed, Mr. Reeve understood what hope really meant.

Alli's optimism and hope, from living life with her cerebral palsy, has encouraged the hope I have in my life. We can rest in hope with the optimism God intends.

? Reflective Questions

1. Where have you lost hope and stopped taking action in your life?

2. How readily and how often do you choose the positive blessings inside the challenges you experience?

⚲ Closing Prayer

*God, my mind and my words say out loud that I have hope in
you, but there are many times I am contradicting myself with
my actions. I want my actions to show my faith in you, God.
No matter what happens to me, I want to walk by faith and
not by sight. I know what Paul says in second Corinthians
about things we see being transitory here on earth, but
what is unseen is eternal, so I, too, will believe in the unseen,
because I want you and eternal life. I want my faith to be
the verb that it is, to be action and forward steps I take. I will
find my hope all the stronger in you the more I seek you in
actionable steps. I want to glorify you, God, in all that I do.
Blessed be your name, God. Amen.*

CHAPTER THREE

Able to Persevere & Be Resilient

Consider it all joy, my brothers, when you encounter various trials, for you know that the testing of your faith produces perseverance. And let perseverance be perfect, so that you may be perfect and complete, lacking in nothing.

† James 1:2-4

As told by Korrine:

When Chad and I got married, we formed a united force of perseverance, but neither of us knew the hurdles we would face ahead. If I ever struggle in my ability to persevere through things, Chad is the person that pushes me to reach deep and strengthen my resilient muscles. And strengthen each other is exactly what we have done through this wild multiple sclerosis journey while raising our family together.

We started our young, married lives in August 2000. I was still finishing my remaining year of college to become a teacher, and Chad was already working full-time as a teacher. After I graduated college, I worked as a teacher's aide and as an assistant. I did this for a couple of school years at two different schools before landing my first official teaching job as a middle school science teacher. The sciences and the medical world have always been areas of interest for me.

We were and are still a married couple interwoven with our vocations as teachers and as coaches. We both have always felt a true calling to this role. We have hearts for teaching, because we care about the well-being of each student from an education standpoint as much as from the character building of each child. As seasoned teachers now, we have many students and their stories forever ingrained on our hearts that will never be written about. Sometimes to do God's work it is best to keep it between God and you.

In the early years of marriage and of forging our journeys in education, I had two distinct and separate events happen that involved my having seizures. One seizure event occurred while I was working with my dad. We were hosing down concrete trucks together and the seizure came out of nowhere. The second seizure event happened while I was out rollerblading with my younger sister, Kate. These events, in and of themselves, were not red flags to me. To an outsider with awareness of what was to come, you might question why two seizure events were not cause for personal concern. I can't explain it other than to say it's just the way I am wired. I wasn't ruffled, because I am not one to be consumed with worry.

While the seizures were not worrisome, a new development of my eyes enlarging and being dilated did prompt me to seek a doctor's consultation. My family doctor ordered a CT scan. This was the first CT scan I had ever had, and the results were clean.

Even though my CT was clean and not indicative of multiple sclerosis, I did have subtle hints from medical professionals that were starting to trickle in my ears. My regular, annual appointments with my gynecologist, my eye doctor, and my family doctor all had similar concerns. They were voicing speculation I might have multiple sclerosis, or MS as we will refer to in this book, based on tiny traits they noticed in their areas of medical expertise. At this time, it was only theory and hunches, though. I didn't allow the prospect of MS to interfere with my active life, so I moved onward knowing I had the clean CT scan. I did not dwell on what-ifs.

Life rolled forward for Chad and me, and with our second wedding anniversary behind us we decided to try to start a family. When we first learned we were expecting, we were ecstatic! We had a firecracker baby on board with a due date of July 4th, 2003. The great gift of a child was pure elation for us. We loved kids and yearned to start a family of our own. The happiness was magnified with two sets of first-time grandparents. Many souls awaited this new life.

Our months of preparing for a newborn were normal; however, our entrance to parenthood with the birth of our firstborn was not what we anticipated. All birth stories are beautiful, because they are glimmers of God's newest creations and gifts, but we went through a very peculiar birth journey to meet God's creation for us.

Being only days away from our July 4th due date, life still carries on, and I had an interview for a new teaching job on Monday, June 30th, 2003. Chad and I were navigating our teaching careers while beginning a family. Logistics and details of jobs and homes, though irrelevant in the grand scheme of life, do play pivotal reasons for the how and why of transpiring events in life. Hindsight seems to reveal clarity on what matters most over the chaos surrounding those trivial logistical details. Such is the case for our wild, first-born child's birth.

My interview for the teaching position was at a school located roughly forty minutes away from where Chad and I were living at the time. The principal was great to interview and talk with, but between answering questions on classroom instruction and conduct, I couldn't stay focused enough to say how I would direct a classroom! It felt like I was having contractions while being interviewed at 2pm in the afternoon with the principal. Being a first-time expecting mom, I was apprehensive about whether labor was really happening. I decided to cut the interview short and start making phone calls. Cell phones were not a life staple at this time, so I was not able to get through to Chad. Next, I tried to call my mom, Gail. Oddly, it was mom who was able to tell me that Chad was already on his way to meet me.

Driving from two different schools and in two different counties, Chad and I convened at my parent's house. From there, we decided to drive to the hospital together in anticipation of our baby's arrival. This was toward yet a different direction than either of us had originated just an hour prior. Little did we know the amount of driving and adventure on our horizon!

It took us longer to drive to the bigger city hospital than it did for my doctor to examine the situation. He quickly deduced that we could be sent home. I was only at 2cm dilation in the labor process, and they wanted me to be at 3cm before admitting me to the hospital. We felt so close to getting to meet our first-born child, yet we understood the instructions and we would do what was needed. The excitement of the afternoon simmered down on our long drive home.

As the last of June's warm, summer evening was closing on our apartment around 8pm I felt a strong resurgence of contractions. This time, I couldn't mistake what was happening to my body. We hopped back in our car together and headed back to the hospital that was forty minutes away.

After arriving and being evaluated a second time, we felt completely deflated when the doctors told us that I had only budged a half a centimeter. I was at a steady 2.5 cm and was not yet to the 3cm they wanted. Recognizing how fatigued I was from enduring contractions all afternoon and evening, the doctor ordered me a sleeping pill. They wanted me to relax. The sleeping pill was administered, so Chad and I journeyed home yet again.

The interstate was becoming a racetrack to which there was no end as we traveled back and forth from home to the hospital multiple times. I was the one technically in physical labor, but Chad was in a different form of labor. His patriarchal duties were sent into over-time on his debut fatherly outing!

The black night enveloping our car ride home could have provided a mellow, sleep-inducing aid to the sleeping pill they gave me, but that was not the case. Instead, I had an unusual effect from the sleeping pill. Rather than encouraging sleep, I was instead in a state of rampant, active hallucinations. I could see vivid, neon-colored butterflies swirling outside my moving car window. This was in the middle of the night, so it was a very dark, night sky, but the butterflies were extremely huge and so gloriously vibrant! Chad says I was thrashing about inside the car. My excitement over the beautiful imagery made me attempt to get out of the moving car window! I wanted to catch the beautiful butterflies that felt like they were within my grasp! Chad was driving at the interstate speed while trying to keep me, a very pregnant and in-labor wife, buckled in the seat next to him.

It was just the two of us on our last adventure before becoming parents! Just like our unique engagement stories, our journey to parenthood was special, too. How many to-be parents can say they needed to keep their pregnant spouse inside a moving car and not chasing neon butterflies outside the window? It's special.

Finally, after sighing in relief that we had arrived home, Chad faced yet another obstacle upon placing our car in park. He had to get an incoherent me up the stairs to access our apartment. We were both tired from the multiple driving trips, so Chad called his mom who lived relatively nearby. Thankfully, she was able to assist and together they managed to get me up the stairs and inside our home. Thinking we would be fine to rest the remaining few hours of the night, Chad's mom went back home.

Looking back at the day I had experienced interviewing for a teaching job with contractions commencing, two full trips to the hospital and home again, topped off with a sleeping pill that I would finally have been able to rest in my own bed at home. Instead of melting into my bed to sleep, I must have plopped on the bed and then proceeded to roll right off it! Chad said I was a sight to see, being fully pregnant and ready to pop, rolling around on the floor. I was in a delirious state and completely unaware of my actions.

For me, the sleeping pill had a long-lasting effect. For Chad, he had to act on his feet to take care of his wife and unborn child, so he called his mom back and asked for help. He made the decision to get me back in the vehicle and back to the hospital. I sure couldn't rest like the doctors had prescribed. Chad was quite fearful of what could happen while I was in that state.

The third trip to the hospital was the charm. Chad secured us a stay for labor and delivery. I remember very little of that third appearance at the hospital, but I do know that Chad was not going to have us turned away again!

I was officially admitted at daybreak on July 1st. I never had fallen asleep from the sleeping pill the night before, so I was in a very physically fatigued state at this point. My contractions continued the rest of the day. From the time my contractions began during the teacher interview the day before, it was over thirty hours later at 8:30pm on July 1st when the doctor made the decision to do a caesarean delivery.

Despite contractions lasting over thirty hours, they did not dilate my body the way it needed. Thus, it prompted the cesarean delivery. Knowing what happened to my mom during my sister Alli's caesarean delivery, I was cognitive enough despite my exhaustion to explain my very serious concerns. I was worried I could have the same effects from anesthetic drugs as my mom during surgical delivery of a child.

The sleeping pill had an amnesia effect on me. Recollecting details of the long hours of labor are difficult, but I do recall the extreme shaking I felt from being icy cold after the caesarean delivery in the surgical room. I just couldn't get warm. My body was in extreme shock and the best way to put it is that I was recalibrating from being in a completely exhausted and depleted state. Post cesarean, I only took Tylenol to combat the pain. It was all worth it, though, to receive the warm bundle of joy into my arms.

We officially welcomed our first son, Carter, on July 1, 2003. Chad and I had been awake since Monday morning and our adventure into parenthood ended with Carter's birth on Tuesday night. Thankfully both sets of those first-time grandparents, as well as lots of aunts and uncles, were there to provide love and support upon the birth.

And as life frequently couples itself with big events, I began my first official teaching position the very next month. I was a middle school science teacher in Vincennes, Indiana for the 2003-2004 school calendar. Ironically, this is not the job I was interviewing for when I went into labor. God directs our paths on His timing, and there's a reason I was placed in this school at this time in my life.

A few months later, I attended a wedding shower with Chad's mom and baby Carter. Loading the car with everything after the festivities, I fastened baby Carter and myself into our seats. Then, I slammed the car door shut. Or so I thought the door was correctly shut, until I realized the door wasn't latched. I had actually shut the car door on my foot. *Ouch!* - should have been the reaction of any of us, but unfortunately it was not my reaction. Immediately, I recognized I didn't feel a thing.

Despite those soft concerns of MS in my history, this was the first time I felt an actual sucker-punch to my stomach. I personally realized something was not right with my body. Could I really have this MS disease? My love of research and science kicked into high gear to pragmatically figure out if what I was experiencing could confirm a diagnosis of MS.

This is the era of time that the internet was building, and I cautiously used it to learn more about MS. There was a priest working in the same school building as me and I shared my concerns about MS with him. He knew I was researching and trying to figure things out. This priest's words still ring in my ears today, "Knowledge can be damning."

During this school year in Vincennes, I was teaching a student whose father was a neurologist. God raised a flag for me. My student's father, the neurologist, in suspecting multiple sclerosis, pursued an MRI for me. When the results of this first official MRI did not indicate multiple sclerosis, a feeling of gratefulness completely blanketed me. I quickly made my way to a little, historic church nearby my school. Alone in the church, I praised and thanked God. I concluded that the news of this clean MRI meant I could exhale with relief at perhaps dodging this MS disease.

When my first school year of teaching concluded, my second school year of teaching middle school science would be at a new school that was closer to home. Chad also would teach at the same school as me, so the 2004-2005 school year felt like a blessing in our lives.

With the change in school environments, I was again feeling those pieces and symptoms of multiple sclerosis nipping at my heels again. Like the doctors shared with me, my signs were tiny pieces and individually, they were only suspect of MS. Therefore, those early, primitive internet searches left me still scratching my head at the real possibility I had the disease. Deciding to be proactive and squelch any of these worries, I sought another neurologist closer to home. They ordered a second MRI that included analyzing my spinal cord as well as my brain. My first MRI focused on my brain, where it is typical to see lesions from MS.

I remember the fateful day I was teaching at school and received the phone call I would never forget. The new doctor's office informed me that this second MRI did in fact indicate multiple sclerosis. I was numb. I didn't want to believe it fully yet. I couldn't deny it, but I needed more confirmation.

My sister, Alli, had previously visited a neurologist in Louisville, whom she thought very highly of, so I made an appointment with this same doctor. I felt in good hands with the competency of this doctor and what he would conclude. He would be able to set things straight for me. I wanted clarity and I had hopes he would give it.

This was the spring of 2005. Chad and I were almost five years into our marriage with our first son a toddler. We were working as teachers and coaches at the same school. It felt like we were settling into a nice groove of life. MS couldn't swoop in and knock us off this worked-for groove. The trip to Louisville felt heavy, as if everything we had established together was about to be rocked.

"You have multiple sclerosis, or MS," were the words confirmed by this second doctor, located in Louisville. Undeniably, he was professional, but he was also very forthright with the hard facts. Continuing in his advisory, straightforward tone, "I would recommend you not have any more children."

These official revelations hit us like a ton of bricks. We were speechless in response to the neurologist. He was relaying to us a medical diagnosis that presumably would impose on our family's plans. It was official, though. I had to acknowledge I had MS. The car ride was a blur with Chad and I crying together on our long drive home from Louisville. Together, through thick or thin, better or worse, sickness or health, we were together. We were building a beautiful life together. We hit a snag in the road with a disease that is known to cause physical disability, but together we grieved and together we moved forward.

MS is the disease which causes the body's immune system to attack the central nervous system. The central nervous system is composed of the brain and spinal cord. MS causes the immune system to assault the myelin coating that protects the axons, or the hardwire connecting one nerve to the next. When hardwires of the nerves are damaged by the immune system's attacks, they form lesions on the brain or spinal cord. The lesions make it difficult for parts of the brain to communicate with each other and with the rest of the central nervous system. Thus, when under 'attack,' the communication is broken down in the central nervous system and parts of the body will be affected. This breakdown, this attack, is called a relapse and it is the progression of MS. MS will progress differently with varying degrees of symptoms in each patient diagnosed with the elusive disease. My journey is uniquely my own as is each person's journey with it.

My first MRI that was ordered by my student's father in Vincennes was looking for lesions on my brain to indicate MS. But, for me, I had an abnormal lesion on my spinal cord. Thus, my lesion was silent and undetected in the first MRI. This lesion on my lumbar spine was the same location that my epidural for Carter's birth was placed. Remember, my MS symptoms progressed after Carter's birth to the point I slammed the car door on my foot without feeling.

We looked at Carter and we felt lucky to have him. Yet, we knew we wanted more children and for Carter to have siblings, too. Through prayer and discernment, Chad and I decided it would be what it was going to be, and if God wanted us to have more children, then we would be blessed. Based on my MS symptoms, and our desire to have more children, we chose a treatment plan with a MS medicine that would allow for a possible future pregnancy. The doctor in Louisville guided and prescribed my first MS medicine shots.

We really wanted to do all we could to show God we wanted more children while also not acting irresponsible in disregarding the MS's presence in my life. Pragmatic optimism and perseverance were the premise of our choice.

My new normal daily routine of living with MS treatment consisted of the daily prescribed shots. I kept teaching middle school science while Chad taught and coached the high school basketball team. Our evenings amid the practices and games also revolved around the amusement of toddler Carter. An official MS diagnosis was not going to dominate my life.

Months turned into a year with no siblings for Carter. Carter was quickly approaching the summer of his second birthday. I remembered the happy tears I had when I knew I was pregnant with Carter. It was such a happy thing and I wanted that feeling again. It felt like it was taking longer, but a day finally arrived when I did get to experience that wonderful feeling of expecting another child. Carter was going to be a big brother! Seeing the positive pregnancy test was an immeasurable gift that followed the bad in my MS diagnosis months prior. Now, my mom might have been the first person to know we were pregnant with our second child. She instinctively knew I was pregnant when we took a family vacation out of state that summer of 2005, and she noticed I failed to have my MS shots along with me!

Carter became a big brother in February of 2006 when we welcomed Rolan into the world. Rolan made us a family of four. It felt great for our family to have the blessing of two sons. But our family of four was very short-lived — in the best of ways!

Ten and a half weeks after Rolan's arrival, I cried those giant tears again looking at a pregnancy test that said I was pregnant! I was completely surprised. After the long wait to conceive Rolan, this was a complete shock. With this unexpected pregnancy, I was still so very happy, but I was also questioning myself on how I was going to handle it all. I leaned on my faith. I knew God had a plan and I trusted that God would give me the grace and fortitude to handle it all. I leaned on God when it felt like too much to handle on my own. I had peace. I knew it was all going to be okay, somehow.

In December 2006, we welcomed a third son we named Tate. Tate is an "Irish Twin" to Rolan because they were born in the same calendar year in 2006. Beginning the new year of 2007, our family consisted of five members and was male dominated. I truly relished and soaked in every tiring minute of being with my boys.

During my pregnancies, my MS had remained in a neutral and managed state. I was blessed while pregnant with MS because for me the MS went dormant. I can say that I felt great during my pregnancies. Now postpartum, I knew I needed to get my MS assessed and treated again. I took a recommendation from someone I knew to see a neurologist in Evansville instead of the neurologist in Louisville who had been the one to confirm my MS case and initially treated me. Evansville seemed like a closer and more feasible fit at the time for me with having the boys.

An underlying and continual theme for both Alli and me is that a journey with a serious medical diagnosis is unceasing, it is daunting, and it is necessary to persevere. Never settling and always seeking another opinion to support the first medical professional's thoughts is sound advice we adhere to. It means no disrespect to any medical professional, but it is in the patient's best interest to double check their diagnosis and advocate for their health.

At this appointment with the Evansville neurologist, I went on a new medicine to control my MS symptoms at the start of 2007. MS is a journey of medicines for each person's unique and specific path with the disease. There is not a set recipe of medicines, nor a set path of treatment for every MS patient.

Chad and I had a lot of discussions to analyze how I felt with my MS and how we felt about the possibility of our family being complete with our three boys, Carter, Rolan, and Tate. These are the same types of conversations every married couple faces with their family planning, but not all couples face the same decision-making while also confronted with the heaviness and uncertainty of a disease like MS. Ultimately, we both wanted more children and Chad especially liked the idea of trying for a little girl to complete our family. We resolved to raise our thoughts for another child with our Evansville neurologist at the next appointment.

This next appointment was in November 2008 with the same doctor who was prescribing my MS meds since the spring of 2007. Our youngest son, Tate, was almost two years old at this point. The Evansville neurologist was rather blasé in her tone and verbal feedback to us. She finally declared, "It's whatever you want. It is your decision and your body. I am not going to tell you that you cannot have more children, because it is your decision."

I was rather vocal in pressing, "How would another pregnancy really affect my MS? I feel on cloud nine while I am pregnant. It's like my MS goes away."

Despite my sincere prodding through different ways of asking, she would nonchalantly state rather simply, "I don't know. I can't answer that for sure."

This doctor could have investigated my situation more thoroughly. She also could have referred me onward to a neurologist who had more expertise in MS, or more specifically, MS with pregnancy. This doctor did neither and I felt zero clarity.

We left the appointment feeling isolated and unsupported, which are sentiments no patient should feel after leaving an important medical appointment. We leaned on each other. We leaned on God. Faith played a factor in my stopping my MS medicine after that disappointing November 2008 neurologist appointment. By ceasing the medicine, I was placed on after Tate's birth, I would be open to a healthy pregnancy for a baby. We tried for only a little while and I was pregnant right away.

Less than a year after the disappointing neurologist appointment, we welcomed our fourth son in September 2009 who we named Kase. We feel this was the path we were meant to follow. This path gifted us with our four boys, and our boys are healthy and happy sons to receive.

A month after Kase was born, I made sure to visit the Evansville neurologist to start back on a MS medicine and ward off any MS progression. I've always tried to be conscientious, proactive, and responsible with the disease, but I also never wanted it to be enabled nor allow it to control my life. I knew the responsible thing was to see my neurologist and get started back on medicine. At this visit I knew our family was complete with my fourth caesarean delivery of Kase. At the fall of 2009 neurologist appointment, I started on a new MS medicine.

A couple months passed since starting this latest regiment of medicine, and I began noticing more MS related symptoms around Christmas time. While the radio belted those jingle bell tunes of bliss and joy, I was feeling anything but merry on the inside. My balance was off, and my back raged like fire. I knew something was dreadfully wrong. It felt like it could be an allergic reaction to the latest medicine I was placed on. I handle pain well. I only needed Tylenol after c-section deliveries, but this was very painful for me.

With the allergic reaction obvious, I abruptly stopped taking the MS medicine and I called my Evansville neurologist. The Evansville doctor's office was not reacting to the dire circumstances of my appeals to them. I felt I needed to be seen right away, because at this point, I wasn't on any MS medicine from having an allergic reaction to my current regiment. With the Christmas holidays, I understood office hours being bleak so I suggested I would take a January appointment. Instead, the neurologist's office told me they were booked up and I would be placed on a waiting list until April's next available appointment.

I was emotionally and physically crushed, but I had to pick myself up and carry on. I had four very young sons I was caring for, including an infant. They needed me and I would not let them down.

A couple more months passed as I waited to be seen. It was now March 2010, and I was inching towards that supposed April opening. The boys were getting bigger and changing. Life was a steady stream of busy and happy, except my symptoms were getting worse. My vision was starting to cause me fits. This was the time my MS was damaging my eyesight. This prompted me to realize I was probably in the middle of a MS event, the progression of the disease, since I wasn't on any medicine.

I went to see my optometrist to get help for my failing vision. The optometrist empathetically looked at me and kindly said, "Look, you have got to go see a neurologist. I can't fix your optic neurosis. I wish I could. I am so sorry, but this is an area I cannot help nor fix for you."

I knew my optometrist was right, and I knew they had my best interests at heart. Yet, I left the office feeling completely disheartened. This was an awakening to how MS was physically robbing my body and my life. I knew my appointment at the Evansville neurologist was less than a month away at this point. Surely, I could manage and limp my way to the appointment I had been begging for since December's allergic reaction to the new medicine. I could persevere until then.

Then, the biggest heartbreak of the situation hit. The Evansville neurologist's office called shortly before my April appointment, and they had to cancel it. Over the phone, I defended myself with dignity, "Look, I need to see the doctor, like now. I needed to see them in January already, and they couldn't get me in."

The voice from the doctor's office thundered inside my adrenaline-pumping chest, "Our next available appointment is in June."

What? My mouth literally dropped. How could a neurologist, who held so much of my future in her hands, cast me to the side in this manner? I felt frustrated, unheard, and exhausted. But above all, I felt abandoned and at a loss for how to move forward. I was emotionally paralyzed. I was teaching full time middle school science with students I loved. I was tending to my husband, our four sons, and our home. How could I possibly keep up with this MS disease if I kept hitting a wall with a doctor who was supposed to be helping me?

So, I stopped. I stopped everything. Six months prior, I had stopped taking the only MS medicine in my possession, because of the allergic reaction. And now I stopped seeing the Evansville neurologist who had failed me.

I took a long pause. This pause lasted all of 2010 and 2011. In Deuteronomy 31:6 it says, "Be strong and steadfast; have no fear or dread of them, for it is the Lord, your God, who marches with you; he will never fail you or forsake you." My faith meant persevering through each day knowing God was near, even though I knew my future was precarious due to MS.

With so much on my plate, I remained as active and healthy as I could. The place I used to be able to clear my head was through carefree running sessions. I had maintained running since those early college days, but slowly my beloved sessions of running were no longer a viable outlet to clear my head. I was no longer steady enough on my feet to run. The realities of my MS were caving in on me and directly affecting my life. Perseverance and resilience will take a person a long distance, but part of being tough is also not being too stubborn to adjust and adapt.

My mom and my mom's sister, Tina, learned of a neurologist who specializes in MS specifically and he was in Houston, Texas. The more they learned the more they were certain that I needed to be seen by this specialist. They knew, as all matriarchs in families can see, that I was busy being an active wife, a mom, and a teacher while trying to circumvent my MS from escalating. Mom and Aunt Tina were my advocates in a time when I needed someone to pull me up.

God knows when our gusto is puttering out of steam. God always provides in a time of need. We just cannot be too inflexible to recognize God's presence in our lives. God works in mysterious ways as well as in the words of our loved ones, like Aunt Tina and mom did for me. This is a beautiful pivoting point, because God steered mom and Aunt Tina, but he also steered Chad and I to be receptive to the help.

Upon calling the new MS neurologist in Houston, it took only 24hrs before Chad and I were boarding a plane to head to an appointment to see him. This was now January of 2012. God's hands were on this visit, though. This doctor was everything we hoped for.

The Houston doctor brought to my attention something new that I was unaware of regarding my MS. In my individual MS situation, I am positive for the JC virus. The JC virus, or John Cunningham virus, is a common germ that doesn't cause problems for a healthy person, but with a weakened immune system, like me with MS, it can be dangerous. The JC virus can interact with certain MS medicines and cause PML, or progressive multifocal leukoencephalopathy, which will infect the brain and cause death. It was a very serious factor to take into consideration when drafting options for my MS.

This doctor's specialization with MS in neurology was apparent. He was an absolute beacon of hope in providing a solid plan for us. I had never felt this type of patient care and this kind of guidance for my MS. And, in this Houston neurologist's consideration of me, he recognized how unfeasible it would be for me to regularly see him, so he laid out options of excellent colleagues of his who were closer in proximity to home. We chose the doctor he recommended who was in Nashville, TN.

The natural proceeding of time meant it was now the springtime of 2012 before I was seen by the Houston neurologist's colleague in Nashville. Two full years had passed since the unfortunate events transpired with the Evansville neurologist. This was what we had waited and prayed for. Chad and my boys needed me. I was not going to let the disease of MS steal me from them. I am Gail Werne's daughter, and I am well-equipped to work hard, to use my intelligence, and to use my grit. My mom is the example of fortitude I want to be.

Driving to Nashville, Chad and I were anxious and very ready to move forward with whatever plans this doctor would propose. His counsel would fall on very receptive ears. It was obvious to us that my MS was progressing. I had given up my favorite hobby in running, but I was still mostly walking on my own. My vision was impaired, and the optometrist had advised they couldn't correct a damaged optic nerve. This was our status.

Sitting in the Nashville doctor's office, our realities and options for the future were clearly outlined for us. This doctor was fully attentive to all considerations including the JC virus. He felt my best option was a drug that was essentially a chemotherapy drug used at that time for cancer patients. It would curtail the disruptions of my nerves leading to the damaged communication in my central nervous system. This ideal chemotherapy drug would control the progression of my MS and curb the gains of my symptoms.

"This really is the best medicine for you, Korrine. I believe it will help you. The problem is that your insurance will deny it because it is a chemotherapy drug." The doctor's voice threw a fast curveball into our excitement with one statement.

This Nashville doctor did not disappoint, but it wasn't to be completely smooth sailing, yet. Is there ever a quick fix in life? Even after all of the struggle and strife with my MS so far, this was not the perfect remedy or fast cure.

The Nashville doctor sent us home on a MS medicine to treat me temporarily until we could get insurance approval for the medicine they really wanted me on. This doctor also promptly wrote a letter to our insurance company arguing for the use of this expensive medicine. He provided examples of many studies proving effective use of this chemo medicine in MS patients like me.

Mirroring the doctor's example, mom, a registered nurse, also wrote a letter to the insurance company when confronted with this new obstacle for us. Surely, between the strong cases made by the doctor, in addition to the case made by the mother of the patient, the insurance company would reconsider approving the medicine. Disappointingly, we were denied again and again citing the rationale of not enough evidence to prove the chemotherapy medicine would be effective for me as an MS patient.

Discouraged but not derailed, we continued fighting and working. With time, the medical field had researched and taken the desired chemotherapy drug, changed a few compounds, and turned it into basically the same drug but in a new structure they could label as a MS medicine instead of a cancer medicine. This became a sister drug to the original chemotherapy drug. It would work for me as a MS patient and for the insurance company. It took years to create it, test it, and prove to insurance companies and the FDA that it was legitimate and good for MS patients. This was time that people like myself didn't necessarily have considering my MS was progressing and deteriorating my body.

It was five full years of staying on top of the insurance company and watching medical trials happen. These cutting-edge medicine trials happened at the same time I needed treatment. The medicine I was placed on during this interim time was not effective. Unfortunately, this further delay in not having access to effective treatment meant an upswing in my MS symptoms. To others, my impaired vision was often an invisible symptom they simply did not know about, but by now I had a very noticeable indication of my MS in the visible use of my walking sticks to walk.

Five years later, the fall of 2017, I finally had all the desired ducks in a row to proceed with a tangible treatment for my MS. I started receiving treatments of the sister drug to the original ideal chemo medicine. This is an intravenous medicine, just like a cancer patient would receive, over a roughly 6-hour session. Reclining in a chair and hooked to the needle and wires of tubes, I watched and waited as the medicine was fully administered into my system slowly and steadily. I do this twice a year as part of my MS treatment plan. My Nashville doctor is still my rock to this date. He has my back and is continuing to guide me in controlling this disease as much as possible.

I was diagnosed with MS in the spring of 2005 when I was around 26 years old. I went on to have three more children while doctoring and living with my MS. For me, the progression of my MS lead to actual MS events, and those events were left untreated through no fault of my own. MS events are uncanny. The events are not necessarily pinpointed, but they are happening. Without a patient-advocating neurologist who specializes in MS, the MS events can prove physically deteriorating, like they have for me. When I finally located the most ideal neurologist in 2012, I had to wait five more years to be treated with the best medicine in my situation.

My MS events altered my life in both visible and invisible ways. My optic nerves in both of my eyes have been damaged beyond current means of repair, so I see blurriness. It's like wanting to always clean your dirty window to see out, but for me there is no cleaning the blurriness away. My eyes also dance and spasm which has a fancy term known as nystagmus. My balance, mobility, and my muscle strength, particularly in my legs, have also decreased, so I utilize a push wheelchair to get around. Since beginning the intravenous, twice a year treatment in 2017, my MS has been controlled.

My journey over the course of nearly two decades with MS has had many struggles and obstacles, but I want to show you that nothing is hopeless if you can persevere with faith. I chose to not give up. It was a God-able choice. Making positive, faith-filled choices yields the fruits of full and happy lives.

I never anticipated my needs becoming like my sister Alli's needs. The extreme irony is that I have joined my sister in living with physical disabilities. And, because I grew up with Alli who handles her disabilities with remarkable class and persistence, I have similar confidence and hope in what my future holds, too. I choose to look at MS as my taking one for the team in our family. I pray God keeps my husband and my boys well as I take on the fight against a disease leaving me physically disabled but my spirit and mind more fine-tuned and God-able.

We all can. We can all be resilient. We can all persevere through struggles. We can be tough, too. God provides the grace needed to have grit to make it through any trial. In Matthew 6:8 it explains how God our Father knows what we need before we ask Him. So, ask God. Talk to Him. God never left my side. He won't leave your side, either. Whether we are asking God or not, He knows our needs, and He has not left us.

We have a choice. Choose to persevere. Choose to be resilient in life.

❓ Reflective Questions

1. What frustrating thing has happened to you in the past, and did you choose to rise above your emotions to persevere through it?

2. What circumstances currently plague you and how will you lean on God to help you be resilient?

🙏 Closing Prayer

God, I know bad things happen in life. I won't live my life unscathed and untouched by this fallen world we live in. No matter what happens, I can be resilient. I can choose to persevere because I have you in my life. If I can try to be resilient, you will lift me up to finish. There will be good things on the other side of my problems and on the other side of my obstacles. Through my struggles and when I arrive on the other side of my strife, I want to glorify you, God, in all that I do. Blessed be your name, God. Amen.

PART TWO

How did we grow to be strong with our physical disabilities?

CHAPTER FOUR

Able to Receive Instruction Humbly

Every act of conscious learning requires the willingness to suffer an injury to one's self-esteem. That is why young children, before they are aware of their own self-importance, learn so easily.

† **Thomas S. Szasz**

As told by Allison:

I have lived for over forty years with cerebral palsy, and I have spent this time on earth working to get the most out of this body I have. This has meant a lifetime of receiving instruction to improve myself mentally, physically, and spiritually. This chapter has been eye-opening and enlightening for me to write, because it has allowed my parents and me a chance to reflect upon the many ways over the years that we tried getting support and improvement for me to reach beyond my CP.

There is one story I want to begin with because it illustrates my personality still to this day. It is also a side to me that few would know based on my physical appearances with my disabilities. This story took place in the fall of 1984 when I was a very young preschool student.

I attended a very happy learning environment at the Southern Indiana Rehab Services, located at the Jasper National Guard Armory. During one school day morning, everyone in the classroom was busy with their activities as one of my teachers stepped out momentarily. She left the door ajar, and my inquisitive nature got the best of me when I decided to follow her. At this time, I had braces securely latched to my legs to provide support as well as a sitting-walker in my grasp. With the braces and the walker, I had independence and I was determined to use it to follow the teacher I loved. My extroverted personality led me astray as I inched down the hall of the armory towards my teacher and straight down a staircase! Thankfully my teacher heard the commotion behind her and made a dash to catch me before I did too much damage to myself. So, as a preschool student, my parents had to be called for me "skipping-class" as a wild child with chuckles about the situation. In all seriousness, my parents were called to inform them that I was okay with no broken bones, and all was considered fine.

This same beloved preschool teacher has shared with me that though I faced many physical challenges it was obvious to her that my mental abilities were right-on. Evidently, I also showed my independent capabilities to my teacher, too! Even though it took me more effort for my body to respond to my intellect, I never gave up because my family never gave up on me. I am a person who acts in life. I was ready to learn both inside and outside the classroom at a very young age!

My parents took a humble perspective to getting me help in life. They kept their minds open as they reached for their goal of helping me improve from my initial CP diagnosis. Likewise, I then had an example and learned to reflect the same actions as my parents towards progress.

A new medical diagnosis, like cerebral palsy or multiple sclerosis, can feel like an entrapment. You can feel caught under the relentless grasp of a diagnosis, because it often has ripple effects to all aspects of your life. It can be dark and lonely. It can feel like a shattering to every blink of the eye as thoughts run from the painful possibilities and well-being of loved ones to the caregiver's responsibilities, to the financial strains and burdens surrounding the diagnosis. Does this new disease imply disability? Does the new disability now imply abnormality in our family? And, in our society, is this abnormality going to hold us back from living life like we always had? Hopelessness and despair can easily be succumbed to.

Regardless of how long the shock from a diagnosis consumes someone, the sun still rises in the east and sets in the west. The earth and everyone else's lives do not stop despite how splintered the new realm of our world feels. The best step to make after a diagnosis, after a setback, and ultimately after circumstances change, is to humble yourself to receive training, collect guidance, and obtain as much development and progress as possible from the new starting point. We need to humbly choose instruction.

"Your daughter will not amount to anything. She probably could be placed in a group home." Those words spoken by a medical professional were given to my parents in 1982 as part of my CP diagnosis. It is now four decades later and I have accomplished so much and still have so much more to give and do. My parents did not allow my disabilities to hinder my life when I was diagnosed by one year of age, and I am still working to not allow my disabilities to hinder my life as an adult.

Mom and dad humbly sought further instruction elsewhere because they would not allow their daughter to be separated from them. Summarizing this to perfection, my mom once simply said, "There's gotta be more than this for Alli. God has more for her." I am grateful to them for their choices.

We started with therapies at the rehabilitation facility in Evansville when I was one year old. This was a first step in a lifelong process. My young, tiny body was influenced by my CP, and direct evidence of this was my "W" style of sitting. The therapists also recognized the logistics of the rehab center being an hour away from home, so they taught mom how to work at home with me to increase my core strength and mobility. Mom took this information and she acted on it. Mom worked with me on therapies at home while my big sister, Korrine, watched and learned. Before long, Korrine was able to help me, too. I gained strength and improved.

In addition to the Evansville Rehab Center, the Shriner's Hospital in St. Louis, Missouri was also instrumental in providing ongoing assistance to me. When I was only a toddler, I began my visits to Shriner's. I still remember vividly the challenging process I endured to receive fitted braces for my legs. It involved casting my legs and sawing the formed cast off to create the braces that would help me. Later in adolescence, I would receive my first automated wheelchair from Shriner's. This hospital was part of my forward progress.

Because of the gains I made by working my therapies at home, by the time I was three years of age I was able to attend two different programs outside of my home daily. This was a sign of success. Personally, it was forward advancement for me. For our united family rallying around me, though, it also symbolized joyful gains to see me attend school with other children.

At three years old, my first daily program began in the mornings with a specialized preschool through Southern Indiana Rehab Services (SIRS) located at the Jasper, Indiana National Guard Armory. The teachers at this specialized preschool were perfect. I grew by leaps and bounds in this loving and supportive environment. The growth was apparent by the confidence I attained in my walking abilities, like when I attempted to explore the armory independently! This program prepared me for the public school system.

My second daily program occupied my afternoons at the Patoka Valley Center for Developmental Disabilities located in Jasper, Indiana. The Patoka Valley Center was a cheerful place for students. Each student had a chart with criteria outlined for their disability needs. The trained staff executed the specific therapies for each child. This is where I received some education, but primarily therapies to develop my crawling, which was the next milestone for me.

A specific way I was taught to crawl was through an activity called patterning. I had to humbly submit myself in the patterning process because I had to physically remain passive and not resist the adults working my spastic limbs. It would take four to five people to hold each of my arms and legs while moving them in the crawling fashion. In essence, patterning was showing me how to crawl while simultaneously manipulating my body to actually do it. It took a lot of daily work to train my body to achieve the same developmental milestones my peers accomplished more naturally and readily. Patoka Valley Center was the ideal environment to cultivate these milestones on my own individual time.

Patoka Valley Center and the SIRS preschool programs were both key aspects of early progress. My family valued both places and supported both as much as they feasibly could. The Patoka Valley Center was primarily funded through the parents and their fundraising efforts, which for one tiny example involved my family selling Christmas trees annually. This extra effort was for the greater good of the entire community of kids at the center. It was merely a byproduct of their commitment to helping me.

I see now how it could be daunting as a parent to approach the task of logistically getting me to and from two different programs daily while also juggling the schedules of their other two daughters and their own jobs. However jam-packed the schedules and tasks were for my parents, they did not allow it to steer them away from helping me. I think when you choose to humbly take yourself out of the equation you are better able to benefit your loved one. To mom and dad, it wasn't about Gail and Terry. It was about prioritizing their family and taking hold of the opportunities available to them. Like James in the Bible says, "God resists the proud but gives grace to the humble." Their commitment to those early programs provided the perfect buoy for me to get to go to public school when I was of age. God's graces carried us there.

I attended public school from kindergarten through the twelfth grade with remarkable, memorable teachers along the way supporting my progress. The greatest teachers were the ones that treated me just like everyone else in the classroom. Through the simple act of being treated like a typical student, I felt important. I tried hard to not allow pride or stubbornness to infiltrate my attitude. I knew my respectful attention in school would better me.

Some of those pivotal teachers in the school system organized the special education students to do Special Olympics. I was so happy to take my adventurous spirit and begin as an athlete thanks to the encouragement and guidance of those positive individuals placed in my life. To begin anything new requires a lowly step to an equilibrium state before you are catapulted in the new endeavor. I did not stay inhibited by my CP. I took my modest, humble start and was propelled to grander heights in Special Olympics.

Through the Evansville rehabilitation center, our dedicated therapies at home, and the learning centers of Patoka Valley Center and SIRS, I developed beyond what the very first doctor's analysis of me had suggested I would attain. Moving onward from the physical improvements, I also needed to increase my communication methods and skills to advance in public school. During my formative adolescent years, mom and dad maneuvered through a great sea of possible opportunities available medically to help me. Discernment was a process as we experienced trial and error. There was no manual that came with me and my CP diagnosis to determine what steps to take, just like there is not a manual provided with any child born to any set of parents. My parents had no personal contacts that they could turn to for help with navigating raising a child with physical disabilities. There was no assurance that each step my parents took would net the desired results, but again this did not deter them from trying.

Progress with a physical disability comes through therapy. Therapy is like a job in which we keep advancing after achieving each tier of work. When we have reaped what we can from one form of therapy, we move forward. The therapy needs to mold to our situation and continue to improve us with newer techniques. My physical disabilities from my CP affected my potential to respond in communication verbally and physically. My brain was affected in the areas of the spasticity in my arms, my impaired speech, and my muscle strength.

For an able-bodied person to communicate with others, the first thing you do is use your verbal speech. I have worked incredibly hard with trained speech therapists to reach my potential verbally. If you have lost your speech like me, similarly to those with the disability of being deaf, you would use your arms and hands to do sign language to talk to others. For me, the spasticity in my arms means it is impossible to communicate in that second option.

Given these obstacles, mom and dad still did not stop searching for a better way for me. They knew I was inside my body and that I needed them to help me come out and live with them more fully. They investigated and searched options to help me.

One of the first places investigated by my family was in Philadelphia, Pennsylvania at The Institute for the Achievement of Human Potential. While there in 1990, we learned of a way to stimulate my brain. The idea was that brain stimulation leads to brain repair and growth, and my brain controlled my muscle function and mobility, so if they could improve my brain function, they could improve my function to communicate and move with them. This technique was done through a breathing mask. The mask strapped onto my face securely containing a plastic baggie with a tube at the end. The technique was to breathe in the bag for sixty second intervals. Of all the positive things we learned at The Institute for the Achievement of Human Potential, this was the biggest takeaway and could be implemented at home. It is important to note that this was also a pivotal moment because mom and dad could have decided to focus more on my physical therapy by following the trajectories at The Institute. By doing so, though, I would be removed from a social, typical school system. These are choices confronted by parents raising a child with physical disabilities. Ultimately, they did what they felt was best for me.

Around the same time as our visit to Philadelphia, we traveled to Fredericksburg, Virginia to learn an Eye Gaze system. This takes an imprint of your iris to run the computer screen. Your eye becomes essentially your computer mouse while you utilize the computer. This proved not effective enough for me to continue using, but this is a real example of trial and error. This was something we tried and learned that it wouldn't work ideally in my situation.

Next, we traveled to Louisville, Kentucky to learn about a dot tracker device. This was like the Eye Gaze system in that its purpose was to help my communication. The dot tracker would be a dot located on my forehead to then navigate the computer and communication devices. This also proved less effective than desired. It's not a failure when we choose to recognize it as part of instruction humbly leading us to something better eventually. One more thing was marked off the list of attempts.

Trial and error proved to us that the most effective device was the use of my head pointer. My occupational therapist crafted my first head pointer during my preschool years. It is an apparatus that is attached via Velcro to my head with a long, extending pointer. It was and is less progressive in nature and possibly could even be considered primitive, but there is a reason traditional things can be ideal. It is classic and it works.

In those early years, before electronics took shape in all our daily lives, I utilized my head pointer and home-made chart boards containing personalized pictures and printed words. I could point my head pointer at a picture or word on the board in my communication attempts. Now, this same head pointer directs a Smartphone and an iPad which have exponentially increased the effectiveness of the original home-made picture boards.

An important aspect to note is that without my fundamental communication skills built through those picture board years, I possibly would not have been able to take the fluid steps into technology. Today, I enjoy using my electronics and consider myself very skilled. I can help those around me with their technological equipment. I am not intimidated by new technology, because I was taught how to learn from early on.

The greatest leap of instruction and thus also the greatest leap of progress for me came in 1998, at almost 17 years of age, when I did a five-week Ability Camp in Canada. This Ability Camp focused on Conductive Education. Conductive Ed for short, has its origins from the eastern European country of Hungary and was developed in 1948 by Dr. Andras Peto. It is a system of learning that improves motor skills for those with impaired mobility resulting from damage or disease to the central nervous system. My cerebral palsy made me an ideal candidate who could benefit from this specific type of program.

Having the limitations I do, I tried with all my might to walk with my walker at the Ability Camp in Canada. I was a teenager and I felt I could better network with my peers and create friendships at the camp if I could simply be up and mobile with them. These are the inner struggles I humbly walk with — literally and metaphorically. Those weeks of instruction in Canada were intense, but they reaped results in increased abilities that I could take home. I came away from Ability Camp in Canada with more confidence in myself and more hope for my future. It was a very pivotal point for me.

Conductive Education can help people of all ages with cerebral palsy, traumatic brain injury, spina bifida, stroke, multiple sclerosis, Parkinson's disease, and those with prematurity and developmental delays. Essentially, this specific therapy is a system of learning that improves motor skills to gain greater independence in daily life. The belief is that what "healthy" children learn through assimilation, children with disabilities can be taught as a skill, and within a compassionate and encouraging environment, students can find their own solutions to their challenges of movement. For me, this was the perfect combination of using my mind and body together to learn.

Conductive Education was a giant leap forward, but unfortunately my family could not gain enough interest locally to get a Conductive Education Program started closer to home. It would have been ideal to have a program near home, one that could help not just me but many others. There was great motivation to continue regular therapy sessions and build on what I had mastered in Canada, but years were unfortunately rolling by. The techniques and therapies we brought home from

Canada were used to the best of our abilities at home. However, they were not nearly as effective, considering they were not in the most ideal setting nor was my family professionally trained themselves to execute the therapies at home.

Our hopes were heightened when we learned about and attended a Conductive Ed program in South Carolina in January of 2009, but only disappointment prevailed again due to the program not taking off fully and from it being simply too far from home.

Shortly after the disappointment, God opened a better door for me to get the therapy I needed. It was February of 2009, a month after our hopes were heightened and crushed and almost ten years had passed since I was first introduced to Conductive Ed in Canada that the Jackson Center for Conductive Ed was opened in Mooresville, Indiana. This is about 2.5 hours from our home, and thus a much better option than South Carolina. I gladly enrolled and have been a loyal and regular attending student ever since. Notice the word use of 'student.' I treat my therapy as a life-long student to continually maintain and improve my abilities, and that is a phenomenal God-ability, to reach into your soul and muster yourself forward with God.

I generally attend Thursday and Friday sessions, which means we typically stay overnight in a nearby hotel to accommodate both days of therapies. Where we regularly stay, the hotel's owners and staff have become an extension to our family, and there is a Mayberry style restaurant where we enjoy country fried steaks. Simply put, this is an additional extension of our lives to travel weekly and receive therapy for me.

Therapy is work. I go regularly, I submit to my therapist's requests, and I give all my effort to improving. Everything I have tried and pursued in the past has set me up for this very specialized therapy and training. The future is unknown, but this is where I need to be for the time being.

Another extension of daily life, in addition to conductive education therapies, is Seal, my CCI (Canine Companion for Independence) dog. I had applied to receive a companion dog in my past, including a time during my challenging school years, but I was never accepted. At a subsequent application in 2013, I was accepted as an adult into the program. The process to receive a CCI is very thorough, formal, and long as it was two years from acceptance until I received my companion for independence dog.

After my application was given the go-ahead, I went through a phone interview and then an on-site interview to determine if I was fully accepted. Finally, I went to the training facility in Ohio to be adequately matched with a trained dog. It took two weeks at the training facility, and ironically the dog I felt most happy with was the dog I was matched to. His name is Seal.

As a CCI dog, Seal is on lease to me. I care for him, but he remains owned by the organization. I continually work on Seal's training to help me. In addition, I have the responsibility to work on Seal's health and well-being. Understanding a CCI dog is something we will discuss further in a later chapter, but the CCI process is part of what it means to accept instruction humbly in the name of self-progress.

My family has been pliable in attempting numerous avenues for my development. If they had been stubborn or resistant to change, I would not be the woman I am today. As a parent, my mom's biggest piece of advice to parents helping a child with disabilities would be to have a proactive mindset. Begin the quest as soon as you learn of a disability, or learn of the change in your circumstance, and explore, investigate, learn, and ask questions. Seek the best options for your child and stand up for their rights. Be positive for them as much as for yourself. In the early formative years, you need to be intense about digging into your own circumstances and finding the best routes to take. Be a patient advocate.

My dad, Terry, has been a steadfast, stable patriarch. When we asked him about his life-time experience of raising a child with physical disabilities and what advice could he offer a young parent faced with the same, dad merely responded with one word — patience. He explains that patience was and continues to be hard, but ultimately that is what it takes. Dad admittedly understands me a lot better now than he did when I was little, but it is still a work in progress even today. What sustains this forward progress is patience along with love.

As the one with the physical disability, I have also had to humbly communicate to my parents about bigger subjects now as an adult in how I would ideally like to be taken care of. This is a humbling and daunting task for an adult individual living with a disability to share formally how their needs will be met. It is hard, but it is an important thing to tackle. Sometimes our bonds become so intertwined that it becomes difficult to voice true feelings and opinions. I took this to task to reflect on my life to my parents. As mom has made recommendations to parents, so too, I have this recommendation for the adult child to share their thoughts and feelings openly and honestly with their parents and caregivers. For me, this meant a written, heart-felt and soul-bearing letter to my parents who care for my physical needs.

The old saying which states *never stop learning* is a motto in my family. My family didn't stop learning when I was only a year old with just a few weeks of therapy instruction at a rehabilitation center in Evansville. They knew I needed an education and worked to see me improving at the Patoka Valley Center and the SIRS preschool program, so that I could be successful in the public school system.

My family was also not pacified with the status of my communication with them, so they didn't stop until my true spirit was able to network with them to the fullest it could be through a head pointer and technology. And, when we learned of Conductive Education and an Ability Camp lasting five weeks in another country, we figured out a way to make it happen. We hope to show what it means to humbly seek instruction, because we still seek weekly Conductive Education therapy.

Abraham Lincoln lived his formative years just over the hills from us in rural southern Indiana. Our family shares the famous president's wisdom that he has been quoted as saying, "I was born, and have ever remained, in the humblest walks of life." Through humbling ourselves, we suffer an injury to our self-esteem like the Thomas Szasz's quote at the beginning of this chapter. Once we swallow our pride, we can accept instruction more readily and easily. Through instruction, the sky is literally the limit to what we can accomplish.

God has seen our paths and helped us find the best help. He's guided the path to where we are now and given us His fruitful abilities. In this life, we all will have issues. Will we choose to be stubborn? Will we ball up in the corner of our bedroom and resist guidance and instruction? Will we research, investigate, and keep learning until we find a way to improve ourselves? Or will we be too obstinate and inflexible to change?

The choice is ours. No one can stop us from learning just like no one can control our reaction to instruction. No matter what our predicament is we can choose to learn to move forward and acquire fruitful God-abilities. We may not be tangibly raising a child who is working through physical disabilities, but through reading about my journey, maybe you can have a bit more perspective of the arduous path it is. For those gaining a better understanding of what it is like to raise a child with a disability, this poem encapsulates this chapter.

Heaven's Very Special Child
A meeting was held quite far from earth!
It's time again for another birth.
Said the angel to the Lord above,
This special child will need much love.

His progress may seem very slow,
Accomplishments he may not show.
And he'll require extra care
From the folks he meets way down there.

He may not run or laugh or play,
His thoughts may seem quite far away.
In many ways he won't adapt
And he'll be known as handicapped.

So let's be careful where he's sent,
We want his life to be content.
Please, Lord, find the parents who
Will do a special job for you.

They may not realize right away
The leading role they're asked to play,
But with this child sent from above
Comes stronger faith and richer love.

And soon they'll know the privilege given
In caring for this gift from heaven,
Their precious charge, so meek and mild,
Is "Heaven's Very Special Child."

By Edna Massionvilla

❓ Reflective Questions

1. In your past, were you a receptive and pliable learner or a rigid, stubborn soul who was resistant to instruction?

2. What issues, no matter their size, are currently plaguing your life, and in what ways can you humble yourself to learn to improve yourself?

🙏 Closing Prayer

God, I am human. My intimate flaws are known to you and me. Despite my blemishes, I do want to improve myself from where I am today. I don't want to remain the same with my body, with my mind, and with my soul. I want to humble myself and recognize that indeed I am nothing without your love, without your support, and without your guiding light. When I most need instruction, please show me. Show me how to improve my body, my mind, and my soul, and in doing so may I bring you glory. Help me to live out the verse from Matthew 18:4 which states, "Whoever humbles himself like this child is the greatest in the kingdom of heaven." I want to glorify you, God, in all that I do. Blessed be your name, God. Amen.

CHAPTER FIVE

Able to Communicate Considerately

God thunders forth marvels with his voice;
he does great things beyond our knowing.

† **Job 37:5**

As told by Allison:

I understand everything you say to me, but you may not understand me.

This is what I normally like to say to someone I first meet. Sometimes I get puzzled looks because I admit it can be difficult to understand me when I talk aloud. When what I say is explained by my sister or mom, who might be with me, often those puzzled looks turn into raised eyebrows of surprise as if they didn't realize I am just as social and friendly as anyone else.

I prefer to think that most people are simply lacking the awareness of how to talk to someone with a physical disability, rather than being so bluntly ignorant that it is only my exterior they are focused on. I really am just an extroverted person who happens to be trapped inside my body with a more limited means of expression — but that doesn't mean I stop trying to communicate. I hope after reading this chapter you will try to be friendly and communicate more often with people who look different than you, too.

The key is to have patience. Meeting me in person, for example, you would see several things. I would most likely have my protruding headgear apparatus on my head. I would have a slight bent of my wavering, spastic elbow high in the air — which I cannot control, try as I might. And my CCI (Canine Companion for Independence) dog, named Seal, would be by my side. My spoken words, admittedly, can be difficult to make sense of — at first. I am like any of us, though, in that we all want to be understood. Some of us will spend an entire lifetime yearning to feel content and understood in our own skin and yet with no disability on our plate to handle. Those of us with physical disabilities maybe hold the keys to the best kept secrets of communication and understanding — and it begins with patience.

Practice the art of patience to avoid the miscommunications which lead to the disappointing things in our life and in the lives of those with whom we interact. I greatly appreciate patience when people listen to me, but I also appreciate it if people repeat back to me what they believe I said. This is full communication when we reiterate what was said. In doing this, everyone has a clear understanding. Had others practiced more patience and more understanding with me, I could have borne a little less disappointment in this life, too. It's our choice to add better skills in our communication tool belt. Make it a priority to receive these fruitful God-abilities.

Memorable Miscommunication in School

With her over-sized sweatshirt, classic of the 1990's, tied around her waist, my big sister Korrine bounced into the special education room to pick me up after the last high school bell rang one afternoon. Korrine was in her senior year of high school, and I looked up to her big time as I was a freshman at the time. Gathering up our trapper keepers and textbooks, we headed out the door with Korrine balancing on the backside of my new automated wheelchair. We were sisters literally on wheels and on a mission even thirty years ago!

We teetered through the network of hallways comprising our open layout of a high school at the time. It felt like a maze to maneuver, but my wheelchair made it a fun and light adventure to conclude a long day of schoolwork. Channeling through a large study hall room we neared the exit to then enter the larger, open locker area when . . . BAM! We hit an abrupt and unexpected roadblock.

I hit the brakes on my wheelchair fast and just in time to avoid hitting our peer teenager in front of us, but Korrine's top half toppled over me before bouncing upright again. Textbooks, notebooks, and pencils scattered to the floor. Korrine & I were stopped dead in our tracks. So much for a light, fun conclusion to the day; it was no longer so carefree. The worn, auburn, carpeted floors of our school served the purpose of buffering any potential wheelchair skid marks as evidence of our encounter. If only the carpeted hallways would have also muffled the further repercussions that unloaded on me.

Adjusting her plaid, flannel shirt, the road-blocked teenager in front of us shifted her hips. Disgust spread across her face as she twisted her scrunchie in her low, messy, ponytail. Squarely facing Korrine and I, she sputtered off, "You f***ing retard!" toward me as I was sitting in my wheelchair.

Maybe I couldn't speak up to apologize for our brief run-in between my wheelchair and this teenager's shins, but I certainly did not deserve the verbal attack I received, either. Korrine went into big sister mode immediately and forcefully put our fellow teenager in her place. She did this in ways you can only imagine a spit-fire Korrine would do. I love my big sister's spunk.

In effect, Korrine put on her armor of God, just like it is talks about in Ephesians 6:11-17 in the Bible. She took a stand firmly against the schemes and forms the devil takes in this world. Her feet were steady with readiness from the years of living her Christianity. She had the breastplate of righteousness and a shield of faith to speak words of truth to this peer of ours who was harboring ugliness. Our peer walked away seeing God's light and truth spoken directly to her through Korrine's words and actions in defense of me. Maybe my presence as someone with physical disabilities was viewed in a new light before she, the foul-mouthed and ill-considerate teen, stormed off in the other direction. At least, I can hope.

Sitting at the end of the hallway, as he often did daily to watch the mingling of students at the conclusion of a school day, was our very seasoned administrator who witnessed the entire scene as it unfolded between the scrunchie-twisting, roadblock teenager and us. This administrator provided us with encouraging, moral support. In his simple way, he gave us an understanding grin of assurance. We felt vindicated. We brushed off the menacing insults and collected ourselves with dignity to continue our way. This encounter was officially a chapter closed and over.

This account was during my first year of high school. I was already faced with an in-your-face kind of adversity stemming from another student's ignorance that turned ugly. There was zero positive communication and zero consideration by the road-blocking teenager in this story. I could not converse back to the teenager in any form whether positive or negative, but Korrine could. Unfortunately, Korrine only shared one year of high school with me before she moved on to college. My communication abilities pre-technology and the lack of patience by those around me would enable further struggles as I continued my high school years.

The Americans with Disabilities Act passed in 1990, and I was in high school in the latter 1990s. Like any change, it takes time for people and organizations to transition and come to accept new and better ways of thinking, functioning, and ultimately adhering to the new law. When I was in high school, the idea of inclusion was not yet a mainstream concept being integrated to its fullest. Combine the lack of inclusion with the fact that technology-advancing, communication devices were not invented yet, it made the late 1990's a rough time for anyone with disabilities to function, especially in a public school system immersed with teenagers.

Teachers would encourage me to mingle with my peers during certain open periods of my high school day. This was very good encouragement, but regrettably I found myself ill-equipped to network with my peers. I had my head pointer but no Smartphone. Cell phones were not a standard personal item of a teenager at the time. If I had the Smartphone I do today, then I know I could have talked for hours with my peers. Very few teenagers walking the halls of the school with me during that time knew that I could talk with them. The mutual understanding simply did not exist. When I tried to talk, they acted like they didn't have the time to talk to me, because they were talking with their own friends. Teenagers would also easily get confused or frustrated with my speech. Ultimately, I mostly sat alone during the allotted hour each day I was supposed to be mingling. There were a few, kind, out-of-the-box thinking students who took the time to know me. They were patient and considerate. I felt heard by those few I could call friends.

If networking with peers was difficult, it was equally disheartening for me to express some things to a few teachers when they became impatient with me. Most of the teachers who crossed my path in school were forms of angels here on earth. They pushed me to succeed at my own pace, but not all teachers have a patient heart throughout every school hour to work with exceptional students. High school and puberty can be difficult to navigate without a physical disability, so essentially the little things morphed into miscommunications for me at times.

A prime example of a simple miscommunication producing immensely hurt feelings for me occurred one afternoon at school. The other students within my regular class were taking a test. I couldn't write my answers down on the papers, so I laid my head down on my desk to remain discreet during the test taking for everyone else. A teacher happened to walk by the open door of my classroom, and she saw me. She motioned with her index finger pointed upwards towards her own chin. I took that to mean I needed to follow this teacher and leave the classroom, so off I buzzed in my wheelchair to head to my special education room. I quickly learned the flaw in my thinking when the teacher corrected me. Evidently, I was supposed to lift my head off the desk and not leave the classroom as I did. I couldn't exactly defend my position nor apologize for misunderstanding what was asked of me, because I was not really given the chance to communicate. I could not speak clearly through my own voice, nor did I have the devices I have today to speak up for myself and explain in the heat of the moment.

I submitted myself to the authority of my teacher and accepted the correction. I was obedient because it was the right thing to do. Sometimes it is far better to not be right, but to still be at peace with our fellow mankind. I can rest in the knowledge that God knows everything. I could be obedient to the teacher because I knew that God saw the whole story.

An example where communication was not the struggle, but rather a lack of consideration, often occurred on Fridays at school for me. Fridays were reward day in the special education room. Movie watching would typically be a favorable reward for most teenagers, but not for a purpose-driven and yearning for independence teenager like me. I wanted the chance to feel of value by doing work or tasks that were needed inside the school walls, even if it was just the job of doing laundry. I would appreciate the opportunity to do a duty, any duty, rather than sitting and watching movies as a reward.

High school years were my chance to develop into a mature adult just like any other high school aged and able-bodied adolescent. My parents both tried to help my independence for me to learn how to deal with my own battles, but in this situation with the movies my mom did speak up for me. She requested work be assigned to me as my own individual form of reward. Communication was open, but consideration was not as readily available. I was told to watch the movies or place my head on my desk. To this day, after decades have passed, I still decline to watch movies. I carry a real disdain for it from watching excessive movies in the form of reward during those formative years in school.

Perhaps what seems as a minor and trivial thing to someone in the moment morphs into a type of scarring and having lasting, negative effects on someone else. Consideration for the other person involved could prevent the unnecessary hurt, like the hurts I had in high school. Do we ever really know the hurt we cause others? Rather the bigger question still rests there to be asked, which is: if we did know the hurt we cause, would we change our words and actions?

Doe Santamat has a poem singing the epitome of what communication means to me. It shares: *It's easy to judge. It's more difficult to understand. Understanding requires compassion, patience, and a willingness to believe that good hearts sometimes choose poor methods. Through judging, we separate. Through understanding, we grow.*

Had individuals practiced considerate communication, perhaps they could have understood me better and grown as individuals. For all of us now, where are we communicative but not considerate? Where are we failing to understand someone else through true listening?

Memorable Miscommunication at Home

I did innumerous therapies growing up, including therapies I could work on at home with my family. Korrine was a primary source of inspiration and motivation for me, and Korrine made me strive to be more than what I thought I could be and do. She pushed me for the better.

We were close with fluid, easy communication between us. It stems from a foundation with a genuine consideration for one another. Playful and friendly teasing exchanged in a good-humored manner is called banter and it is often found between family members who are driving each other in a forward manner. Whether banter between siblings is there to edge the other in physical activities or to correct them on subpar actions, banter happens out of consideration for another family member. My family has a lot of positive banter. We love it.

Banter was also a part of our at-home therapy. Some of our family therapy sessions involved outside time in the pool. Whether it seems ridiculous or not to see one sister pull a physically disabled sister to the bottom of the pool, it was exactly the type of exercise I enjoyed with Korrine! After towing me to the bottom of our pool, Korrine would release me to kick my way to the top. Trust existed between us. There was a mutual understanding. Korrine knew I enjoyed the water exercise and the challenge of kicking myself to the top of the pool. Likewise, I knew I was in a safe place to push myself past my fears. It wasn't torture or any form of induced infliction. Instead, it was an endorphin-attaining pleasure for me to discover new levels of my abilities. When I was in the pool, my disabilities felt weightless. The pool has always provided me with limitless potential to shine my physical gifts. To this day, I like to compete in swimming heats at Special Olympics.

From the pool to the indoors, Korrine would push me to use my arms and my legs in all areas of physical exercise. With braces on my arms and the walker square in front of me, I practiced walking regularly during those years while we were growing up together. I loved and wanted to please my older sister, so I worked especially hard with Korrine.

Even when a bond is as close as it is with us, the deepest things we sometimes think and feel can still remain hidden. These hidden things are not intended to be secrets, but they bypass any out-right communication due to a polite consideration and respect for one another. In reminding ourselves if a comment is true, kind, or necessary, we opt to merely resolve some of those feelings within ourselves instead of projecting them outward. Having these less than stellar thoughts and feelings, lacking in necessity to be said, is not wrong. Expressing them however can be wrong if in the wrong context. I have an example to share on this idea.

I also want to normalize these natural human flaws that are lingering as hidden feelings to comprehend how far the true love of God and His mercy can carry us. God's love and guidance within our families is sacred because the family is God's masterpiece. It takes communication with one another at the right time and within God's sphere and His circle of protection to feel free of these natural human flaws and feelings. In other words, there is a correct time to share true feelings with another family member and feel protected by God's love, mercy, and His reconciliation and redemption of those thoughts.

I had one such physical therapy session with Korrine, decades ago, when we were both older teenagers. In this story, my natural human feelings were never fully communicated in the moment. I took captive those thoughts and feelings ever so tightly within my soul for all these years until a chance came to reconcile them.

I had been making great gains in my walker one summer. Standing upright on my own two legs I was making my steps back and forth across the length of our ranch home's living room floor. With Korrine cheering me on, I would take even more steps to delight Korrine. I was reaching my potential for the day, but Korrine sought more than what I could communicate was my maximum contribution. I know Korrine pushes me for the betterment of me, but I became frustrated. I became fatigued. I became a little angered in the heat of my exhaustion and inability to communicate it in the moment to her.

"Come on Alli, you got it in you. I believe in you. I know you can do this," rang Korrine's sweet coaching words.

Not able to fully communicate exactly what I was feeling, I tried to reach within myself and finish what Korrine was asking of me.

"This is awesome, Alli. You are totally doing this. You are walking so well. I am so proud of you!"

My mind was maxed out. My body was also depleting fast. How could I ever continue? Would I disappoint Korrine if I stopped? Would Korrine ever understand this was enough for today? I dug deep, really deep within myself. I could conquer pool time excursions to the bottom of the pool, but this, this was different. Why was it so different? I couldn't explain it, but it was somehow different, though.

Korrine's cheerful attitude for this one random occasion was not benefitting me. I couldn't bring myself forward any more steps. I felt done, but even more so I felt defeated at the trajectory of the therapy for that afternoon. I was frustrated at my inability to convey to Korrine that I was actually and truly done. The feelings of physical exhaustion and emotional frustration will blend to create anger in anyone, and my emotions were heating inside me.

I slumped into my wheelchair, hung my head, and closed my eyes. Finally reading my physical cues, Korrine provided wonderful sisterly compassion saying, "It is okay, Alli. You did good for today. You worked hard. We'll call it a day on exercising. The time is flying anyways this afternoon, and I need to make a lunch before I must leave for work."

Korrine headed to the kitchen to make a quick snack before heading to her lifeguarding job at the local pool. Watching busy Korrine from across the room, I reflected further as I sat in my wheelchair. Being trapped inside your body provides abnormal amounts of time inside one's thoughts. Self-reflection and the thoughtful exercise of analyzing the lives of those around us is a honed skill of mine. I read body language well. It is both a blessing and a curse.

My thoughts flashed all over the place. I love both of my sisters. They support me. They include me. They are interested in what I like, what I don't like, and what I really want. They cheer me up on days I am blue from my disabilities. Korrine and Kate share their lives with me, and they desire my thoughts and inputs. Yet, this was a small moment when my natural human feelings engulfed my spirit. Would my sisters ever really understand what it is like to live in a wheelchair like me? I had never once thought they should feel what it feels like, until that very moment.

Just this once — this one time, I wished Korrine could know exactly what it was like to be confined to a wheelchair. If she was in the wheelchair, then maybe Korrine could feel just how much it hurt me this day to be worked so hard in physical therapy. I wished Korrine could feel my despair and hopelessness.

The encouragement Korrine always provided was put aside. I hurt physically but I realized that I was hurting more emotionally. I hid these feelings. Korrine could not see these concealed hurts. Even with immense amounts of understanding in place, and even with positive communication and positive banter, negative humanity creeps into play in all of us at any given point in time. It is part of the natural realm we live in, a fallen world.

There was no way I would express in the moment that I wished my then-able-bodied sister, who was bouncing all over the kitchen making a sandwich before getting to go to work, was in the wheelchair like me. I would not take my ill-thoughts in a wrong action by expressing them. My Christianity told me to stop and take those thoughts captive. I contained those once-felt, ill thoughts and feelings for years — for decades.

Then the irony of it all came crashing to a peak because the day came when my beloved, big sister Korrine knew what a wheelchair felt like. I was completely devastated. I privately reflected on everything. Did my human-flawed thoughts result in this outcome? Could I possibly have anything to do with Korrine's MS diagnosis and the progression of her disease? Why did the events unfold like this? This was not fair. This is not what I ever genuinely wanted nor desired. Those bad thoughts and feelings were not real, were they?

In the safe place within God's loving presence, I had the opportunity to fully communicate to Korrine. Life now had us both sitting in wheelchairs at Korrine's kitchen table discussing our lives with Laura for this book. It felt like a safe place and time to share. I had a grievous cloud hovering over my soul, and I felt it was time to be absolved of it. I wanted to be free, and I wanted Korrine to know that I truly didn't want her in a wheelchair like me.

Mustering extreme courage, I spoke up. I used my words and the use of my iPad's verbal connections. "I did, Korrine. I did wish you could be like me, so that you would understand what it feels like to be in a wheelchair, impaired, and working hard. I meant it." Merciful tears were flowing from my eyes as I continued in my own speech to express my immense sorrow. "I am so sorry, Korrine. I meant it then, but I don't want it now."

We were in a circle of what felt like heavenly communication between us sisters and our mom. There was not a dry eye around our kitchen table. We had tears of surrender, tears of love, tears of reconciliation and absolution, and ultimately, tears of complete understanding and mercy. Korrine broke our prevalent crying with her typical gusto, "I wouldn't change it for the world. I am fine. I am more than fine. I am good. Alli, it is okay!"

I felt the need to ask, "Did you know, Korrine, that I wished this all those years ago?"

Korrine replied, "Nope, I didn't know it, and I don't think a thing about it because it is human nature. It is fine. You were mad at me for making you work so hard on your therapy!"

Mom comforted both of us. The amount of love exuding from our mom is one of the reasons I think she is comparable to a saint. In her years of hard-earned wisdom, mom was able to speak God's truth. "God doesn't do things like that, Alli. God didn't put Korrine in a wheelchair because you wished it. This was all part of God's plan from the beginning. He knew everything before we did."

Mom spoke the truth because she identified with God forming us in our mother's wombs and the supreme foresight God has in what He creates. In Psalm 139:13-16 it says: "You formed my inmost being; you knit me in my mother's womb. I praise you because I am wonderfully made; wonderful are your works! My very self you know. My bones are not hidden from you, when I was being made in secret, fashioned in the depths of the earth. Your eyes saw me unformed; in your book all are written down; my days were shaped, before one came to be."

God's plan for us was and continues to be known to Him. And, because of our constant seeking of Him, He reveals Himself and His plans to us little by little. In James in the Bible, it says to draw near to God and God will draw near to you. For us, too, we can draw near to God and He will draw nearer. I'm not just talking about Mom, Korrine, and I, I am talking about you, too. For all of us, we have a chance to draw closer to Him.

We try to communicate. We try to listen. We try to understand. And what we fail to communicate and understand is covered eventually with God's loving mercy. We all have a choice of when to speak and how to speak. Choose temperate and pleasant tones with kind words when it is necessary to speak up. Always speak from a place of consideration and compassion for others. God's grace will be sufficient for us, and He will supply His God-abilities for us. Remember, when we are most misunderstood, there is an omnipotent God who knows us, understands everything about us, and above all else, loves us.

❓ Reflective Questions

1. When was a time your gut told you to speak up for what was right, and you failed to do so?

2. Especially thinking of a loved one, in what ways can you prepare yourself to communicate truth in a considerate manner to bring healing to both?

🙏 Closing Prayer

God help me to live more temperately. I desire your wisdom to equip me in my daily walk in this life. Help me understand the people who cross my path today. Let me be considerate of who they are and of how they may feel. I need your patience and your mercy. I ask that you guide my words to communicate effectively and kindly. I want to draw my strength from your heavenly power and only radiate your pure and holy love in the world around me. I want to glorify you, God, in all that I do. Blessed be your name, God. Amen.

CHAPTER SIX

Able to See Your Purpose

*We must listen, often for a long time, but there
are also opportunities to say with words or simple
gestures: 'Didn't you know that what you are
complaining about can also be lived as a way to
something new?' Maybe it is impossible to change
what has happened to you, but you are still free to
choose how to live it.*

† **Henri J.M. Nouwen in
"With Burning Hearts: A Meditation
on the Eucharistic Life"**

As told by Korrine about Allison:

I will be the first and the loudest person to tell you that my sister
Allison's entire life is a lesson to all of us. Her purpose here on earth
is to teach us. She shows us by her shear example the fruitful life she
has from living her entire life with cerebral palsy. I might be busy as
a wife, mom, and teacher, but I can tell you that my journey with MS
and the physical disabilities that have come my way are fruitful in large
part because of Alli. I draw strength from her. I draw strength to find
the fruits in my life, because I know that is what she is doing in her life.

Allison has shared of our physical therapy sessions at home together,
but I want to share with you how hard Alli still works now as an adult.
If Alli stopped moving and stopped working on her body, she would

stiffen from her CP. Allison works every single day at doing therapies to increase her independence and her ability to provide self-care. How could I not keep working on myself to find the good I can still do when my sister hasn't stopped working on herself since the beginning?

Here is a recent depiction of her immense efforts at a therapy session at the Jackson Center for Conductive Education in Mooresville, Indiana.

"Good. Good. A little more, a little further, you are doing it. Nice. Nice. Nice," rings the soothing and assuring voice of Edit, the conductor of Alli's Conductive Ed therapy. Edit has worked with Alli and her therapy in adulthood for over a decade now. She pushes Alli just like I used to do.

Knees bent on the colorful mat below her, Alli shifts her body upright next to a yellow exercise ball that is equal to her in size. Hearing Edit's encouragement propels Alli to crunch her face in the same manner I see NFL quarterbacks do before executing those fourth and goal plays. All Alli's might is in steadying her ever-swaying, spastic arms and in using her abdominal muscles to support herself to an erect position and hold it there. Bystanders of Alli's therapy always remark to us that Alli must have abs of steel to complete the challenges.

Alli's CP, for her specifically, means she needs some assistance to stand and sit, and her arms are difficult to manage with their spastic movements. This exercise with Edit can be daunting. No matter how much Alli wills it, her brain cannot get her body to immediately do exactly what she wants and needs. Wanting precision and perfection, Alli works with determination and pushes through this obstacle in therapy.

She rolls her body over the exercise ball. Her arms are stretching, reaching, and pulling her upper body higher and over the ball while balancing atop it. Moving forward with each step she does is done with sheer strength. Then, she rolls herself just as methodically back to her original position again.

"Good job, Alli," Edit shares as she grabs Alli by her waist to secure her. This signals the completion of this round of exercise. The entire task of rolling her body over the large exercise ball and back again transpires with a quiet pace.

Next, Edit assists as Alli is brought to her feet in a standing position behind the same yellow exercise ball. The buoyancy of the ball makes it fickle for Alli to gain hold of it. Leaning forward, Alli is deliberately stabilizing herself, stabilizing her swinging arms and stabilizing her upper body, while simultaneously reaching and grasping for the ball. It almost escapes her, but Alli is quick in her reflexes to keep it.

With her bright, blue, fitted top and her Capri-leggings, Alli's attire aligns her with the visual façade of an athlete, but her true traits as an athlete are shown as she works these exercises with grace and grit. Wobbling like a new fawn, Alli's resilience results in finally bracing the large, yellow exercise ball.

"I'm going to let you go now," Edit acknowledges Alli's indication that she is sound enough. Again, holding the ball securely, balancing her body, Alli rolls slightly forward with the ball, while arching her back and bending from her now standing position.

"It is time. All the way up, all the way back up; keep coming," Edit shares aloud. She is supporting Alli's ability to boost herself from the ball back to an upright standing position. Looking upwards, Alli sees the natural sunlight pouring in from the large windows of the Jackson Center. All around her are brightly colored stations of therapy and independent learning centers. This place is a beacon and a literal light for Alli.

Standing upright in front of Edit, Alli flashes her killer smile, melting anyone's heart who watched her in this yellow exercise ball therapy. The feat was accomplished on this exercise! But this is only one exercise of the many Alli will do on a daily session of Conductive Ed therapy.

This scene happens now currently. Alli is an adult and her therapies come in many different forms, but she never grows lax or lazy on them. Therapy with a disability is like having a job in that you keep rising within the ranks, within the ever more challenging exercises and tasks. How many of us can say the same? Do we honestly take care of and try to improve our health daily? Do we work this intensely hard with the body we have? Because of her dedication to the work, Alli does maximize the body God gave her. This is what I call fruitfulness and purpose.

This on-going therapy is vital to Alli's agility, mobility, and quality of life. Alli deals with bouts of chronic pains in her back from the long-term effects of living with CP. Even with therapy, the chronic pains can be hard to manage, particularly in the cold winter months. Individuals living with CP have a harder time regulating their body temperature and it is not uncommon to have uncontrollable muscle spasms. While Alli struggles with the cold, I struggle in the heat because the summer heat melts my MS body like Jell-o.

For Alli though, another method of aid in managing this chronic pain has been myofascial release administered by a therapist. Alli also appreciates growing her own herbs in her raised garden beds. She especially likes to grow sage herself because the quality is better than what she can find at the store. She uses sage in her daily diet to ease her muscle spasticity. Alli is always researching ways for the both of us to help our bodies heal and improve. I appreciate that immensely.

On another afternoon at the Jackson Center, Alli was doing a therapy session with a college student working as an intern. The student voiced confusion over her discernment for the best course for her future. She was debating whether she should pursue her medical training as a nurse or as a therapist. In Alli's powerful way, she spoke wise words of truths to this student. Alli said that the student should ask herself if she prefers helping others or if she prefers helping others learn how to help themselves. Put bluntly, nursing is caring for people whereas therapy is helping people learn to care for themselves. This is also an example of Alli's ability to use her wisdom to help and teach others as part of her purpose.

Along the way through the years of on-going therapy, Alli ran into a roadblock with her health insurance. They were dragging their feet on whether to pay her therapy sessions and were proposing to halt her needed therapeutic services altogether. Insurance felt that Alli's CP meant her brain was permanently damaged and the therapy would thus not improve her situation. This felt very demoralizing.

Alli had to appeal her insurance company on the claims. From her appeal, they invited her to come before them on a panel to state her case. Alli's therapists joined her cause, and an intern even helped Alli to research the component of the brain pertaining to its continual growth. The fact that a human brain continually grows would illustrate how therapy aids the personal gains of individuals working a therapy program. From their joint efforts, Alli herself then composed a letter which she had read by her iPad aloud to the insurance panel at the formal meeting. This in-person meeting left the insurance panel speechless to realize Alli's abilities. It prompted them to inquire of the therapist accompanying Alli if the letter was written by Alli or the therapist. To their surprise, the therapist confirmed it was done by Alli.

In the end, Alli proved her therapy was beneficial. Sadly, Alli had to go through unnecessary steps to prove the function and improvement of her brain to get her needed on-going help. This is another instance of Alli being trapped inside her body and having to surge with all her might to the surface in conveying herself to others. This insurance story demonstrates Alli's resilience in adversity, and therein also lies so much of Alli's purpose in life, too. Her life is a living example to everyone she encounters of how to live with more hope, more strength, more resilience, and especially more love in our hearts.

I am a teacher by trade, but few know that my sister Alli would like to have been a teacher herself. Being a teacher in the typical means of leading a classroom filled with students is perhaps not what God has planned for Alli. Rather, Alli's entire life is a form of teaching character virtues to the multitudes of people around her — including those who know her personally and those who know her from afar and watch her in action.

Special Olympics have been a steadfast source where Alli has found achievement, success, and purpose since she began the competitions at the age of eight. While regional and state games might be held on their respective singular weekends, the training and practices for various sports comprising the Special Olympics Games are held throughout the entire calendar year. As a young child, Alli began the competitions doing what she was able to do at the time, which included rolling in her wheelchair and crawling events. She advanced to doing a tennis ball throwing event and eventually onward to swimming competitions. Swimming is where she has thoroughly enjoyed the challenge of sport and competition. Our youngest sister, Kate, and I have tried to support Alli throughout her Special Olympic competitions.

Alli took her years of participation in Special Olympics to a higher level by being a member of the local ALP's chapter, or Athlete Leadership Program. ALP's meet regularly throughout the year and support the mission of Special Olympics while in their leadership capacity and role. Alli helps others through her involvement in the ALP's.

In 2006, Alli was invited to give a motivational speech to 1500 new employees of the French Lick Resort Casino in historic French Lick, Indiana prior to their grand opening. This event included an Olympic style torch run in addition to her important speech. In 2007, Alli won the Indiana Special Olympics Athlete of the Year for her area, warranting an acceptance speech during a banquet ceremony. And, in November 2012, Alli provided a keynote speech at the National Convention for the National Fraternal Order of Police by representing Special Olympics.

Alli is also beloved in our local community. People see her resounding purpose in being who she is — the hardworking, ever-loving, young lady who teaches everyone so much about life. Several individuals in our community sought her recognition by nominating her for a special award, and in 2006 Alli received the Indiana Young Hoosier Award through the Jaycees. During a ceremony in Brown County, Indiana,

Alli had a beautiful and very well-deserved light shone upon her. In addition, Alli and Mom were recognized in our church by being the Simon Bruté recipients. It is an honorary association of lay persons for their outstanding example of Christian stewardship.

Alli doesn't stop. She's given speeches. She's competed in hundreds of sports competitions. She's won awards. She's discovered hobbies of painting, technology, and sewing on her sewing machine. To this date, Alli is still learning new skills. She is pushing her brain and her body to work together in doing things an able-bodied person takes for granted, like personal care and feeding oneself. Every single day Alli works to attempt these things. Her positive outlook despite what she cannot have on impulse and demand is a lesson. She's a daughter, a sister, an aunt, a friend, and more importantly she is a sister in Christ to anyone she meets. This is Alli's loving purpose. Her life is a lesson in love. Alli loves us by showing us her example. Didn't Christ do similarly with His life by showing us examples of love? Finding our purpose is cliché. Our purpose finds us while we are actively progressing and moving forward in life. We realize our purpose while we are allowing our free-will to meet God's holy-will for us. Allison is doing it. Let's follow her example.

As told by Allison about Korrine:

My big sister, Korrine, has the biggest heart. She uses her incredibly compassionate heart to guide her own kids and the many children she helps as a teacher. She uses her huge heart to help me stay focused on the positives of things. I want to share some wonderful stories of how my big sister lives and shows love through her purpose in the daily things.

A few years ago while on a regular weekend shopping excursion, Korrine was happily browsing the busy Christmas season aisles and attempting to keep track of her lively crew of boys. There are four of them! Shopping at a large box-store with energetic boys is like corralling cats, but it is nothing out of the ordinary for Korrine. Raising boys means each day becomes an adventure. When the boys were much younger, the adventures involved a lot of mud, puke, poop, blood, nature, dirt, and still more mud. There are many of those types of stories!

Few things surprise this seasoned mom but rounding the endcap of an aisle was a display of over-sized, stuffed penguins. This display was catching the boys' attention with thunderous merriment. Their fun, uncensored loudness never had fazed Korrine. She was, however, shocked by just how much joy the large penguins huddled together in the bungee-corded enclosure brought my nephews. The penguins were the size of Korrine's youngest school-aged son at the time. The stuffed guy had a lot of personality that evidently was the draw, with his orange, webbed feet, and his bright orange little beak atop his monstrous head. The boys found some unique happiness within their daily adventure.

Later in the evening after returning home from the shopping trip, Korrine and Chad had an honest conversation with their boys regarding Christmas expectations for that year's impending holiday season. Their youngest shared his truth of heart in feeling like Santa seldom follows his wish list for Christmas. He exclaimed that all he really wanted for Christmas that year was the penguin they saw at the large box-store that afternoon! Of course, the little things are the big things, and it was duly noted as he scampered off.

After he left, mom and dad had a chance to hear their older sons in a more adult conversation regarding their wishes for Santa. Each of their older boys voiced the same thing. They had recently moved into their new home and were ecstatic with it. They genuinely appreciated everything they had and wished for nothing more. Again, the little things are the big things, of course. All four Whitehead sons illustrated this simple fact in different ways, and it brought delight to their parents.

Thinking of her youngest son's longing for the random and unique penguin made Korrine jump into a mom-on-a-mission mode, and her loving mother-in-law, Phyllis, was her cohort on this important mission. They knew it was too late to send Santa a last-minute request for a certain, large, stuffed penguin, so they took matters into their own hands. They made it their mission to get that penguin by Christmas!

The next day, they went back to the same store to find it. Searching the store, their hearts were racing with each bleak, empty aisle. The penguins were not in the same place in the store and Korrine was very fearful they were all sold out. *Seriously,* she thought to herself, this many people wanted a penguin this large was odd. Finally, she found a manager and asked where the penguins were stashed that were on display just the day before. Ah-ha! He knew of one, and only one, that remained, and it was hidden in the back. He went to fetch it for Korrine and Phyllis. Mission accomplished! This would be the best Christmas to date for her youngest son!

Indeed, as God intended, Korrine is the perfect mom for each of her boys. She understands each of them. The penguin was officially given the affectionate name of Joey, because he needed a name to feel like he belonged in the Whitehead family of course, too. On the exterior this outrageous penguin represents a little boy's Christmas wish come true. But more than that, it represented a mother's love, attention, and care for each of her sons.

Korrine was born to be a mother, and she was also born to be a teacher. Korrine understands her purpose because she loves and welcomes children the same way Jesus loved and welcomed children. Both purposes revolve around children.

In school, students find purpose in belonging by being part of the school family that Korrine welcomes them into. Korrine brings self-worth, dignity, and purpose out of each child she works with. Because Korrine shows students it is ok to struggle, they are then eager to try more. Students strive for their own respective potential through Korrine's example that demonstrates encouragement and support.

At times, a pack of children can be seen huddled together like a football team meshing about while walking down the long corridors of the elementary school where Korrine works. At first glance, this scene can appear as though no adult is accompanying the large gang of young children moving about the halls. But, upon a closer look, it is revealed that a fellow teacher, Korrine, is smack dab in the middle of the pack of students rolling in her wheelchair. There is a halo of glowing happiness that rises above this huddle of children and Korrine. As they make their way up and down the long halls, it is evident to colleagues that Korrine is a magnet to children. And she fills the kids with the attention and love that every child needs. It is a beautiful sight.

Some school mornings are hard for students. They don't want to go to school and have trepidations and fears. Then a rare opportunity, in the form of Korrine in her wheelchair, zooms over to the car containing the hesitant child. Korrine allows the child to push her in the wheelchair into the school and accompany her until the child feels warmed up to be at school. Through this experience the child finds purpose, finds belonging, and finds sparks of joy. Their reluctance about school slowly shifts away as they find a subtle reason to be at school.

Inside a classroom, Korrine can be found clustered up with students for instruction. Korrine's sight is impaired, but she uses her weakness to bring the strength out of the students. She becomes the blanket of comfort they need to work through their own struggles. Korrine's vision impairment is not something easily noticeable about her, so it becomes a personal thing to become aware of it. The students eventually forget their questions about Korrine's eyesight and instead they soften into the warmth she exudes and the instruction she provides.

When Korrine arrives in a classroom with her big personality and positive attitude, the feelings of ineptness at topics like reading are sucked out of the classroom. Students regularly see someone in a wheelchair whom they admire. It erases the stigma that being in a wheelchair is a bad thing. The weight of Korrine's presence in a school setting to promote inclusiveness and kindness towards those with a physical disability is pure gold.

Korrine wasn't always popping wheelies with a wheelchair and using magnifying apparatuses to teach her students. She began teaching completely able-bodied and without an MS diagnosis. She guided students individually because she cared. Students were shown that they were seen in this world by the sincere attention and empathetic love Korrine gave from a place of dignity and respect. To this day, Korrine has lasting bonds with students from decades ago.

Korrine's many years of leading her own classroom have prepared her for how she now works with students — through enrichment and intervention, while also assisting her husband in his administrative position. She cares deeply about the students. She carries them home with her on her heart. She prays for them, and then she ultimately comes home to give her full attention to her own boys as a mom.

Teacher and mom — these are Korrine's purposes.

Her body fails her due to her MS, but it doesn't stop her from living her purpose. At the end of most days, she meanders into each of her boys' two, shared bedrooms and makes sure to connect with each one. Exhausted physically and emotionally from pouring herself into students all day and then pouring herself into her children and husband upon returning home, she still consents to her youngest son's wishes that she crawl up in bed with him and snuggle. Her spiritual being is not exhausted. She will not become stagnant or idle in the care of her spirit. Her spirit has the strength to finish the day giving the last ounces of love to her kids and husband.

Grabbing the bedpost and mustering strength, Korrine wearily stands up out of her push-chair and catapults her body into the bed with her youngest son. He is happy to assist his mom's endeavor to crawl into his bed with him and have snuggle time. With her hand already on the wooden bedpost, she also grabs the corded rosary hanging there. The corded rosary is symbolic of a routine of love. It is time to pray together, time to connect, and time for her son to be seen and valued. Oh, and Joey, the large and happy penguin from several Christmas's ago, is there in bed as well.

As shared by Gail:

Our destination throughout life is to strive and work to get to heaven. Work, effort, movement forward, however you wish to describe it, we are all on a mission to get to heaven. We are broken and on this journey to eternal life together. Our purpose is to take our free-will and unite it to God's holy will. It is as complex and over-thought as we want to make it. Move towards Him and we are successful in life. Move towards Him and we find our purpose. Move towards Him and we will find our fulfillment and peace.

We are given our own soul and our own free-will, no matter what comprises the outside shells of the bodies we carry around on this earth. Disabilities like what Alli and Korrine live with are just their shells, not their souls. Their purposes shine brilliantly and more purely from within. Look at Korrine and Alli — they see themselves and happily share that they are sisters, partners in crime, while on wheels! I love how all three of my daughters support each other to see their purposes.

Dr. Greg Bottaro says in his book, Mindful Catholic, "Your happiness is directly connected to you becoming more of who God made you to be." We decided as a family not to ask, "Why us?" Instead, we decided that there is a reason that *it is us*. We own it and accept it. Our theory is that someone somewhere is suffering more than we are, so we choose to not complain nor wallow in self-pity. This propels us to a positive place.

The day we give in and stop trying and stop taking action becomes the day we start losing hope. We live by the mantra that we all need to just keep moving to get where we want to go! ACTION! Sometimes my daughters must crawl, but they keep moving. We can be robbed of many things in life, especially with physical disabilities, but no one can take away our hope. It's OURS!

Hope to us is also an acronym that stands for hard work, optimism, persistence, and enthusiasm. This is something we believe in deeply and wish to share as much as possible. We recognize our very presence in public, like attending all the youth sporting events, is a beacon of hope for some people's paths we are blessed to cross. We view it as an opportunity when we are in public. We know we get looks and stares, so why not share our optimism regarding our own situations with others. Korrine and Alli echo what famous gymnast, aerialist and author of *Everything is Possible,* Jennifer Bricker-Bauer, says: "If you catch people's attention, use that attention to educate, inform, and inspire others. In essence, this becomes a purpose in daily life."

Be patient with an open heart and open mind and you will see a fruitful realization of your purpose. Half of the struggle in recognizing our purpose is in first realizing our worth in who we are as a person. Our worth is derived in being a child of God first and foremost in this world. As St. Benedict says, "Listen with the ear of your heart" and be guided by God.

Let's realize our purpose all along was simply to dwell with Him now so that we can dwell with Him later, in heaven.

❓ Reflective Questions

1. In your over-thinking power-struggle, do you stubbornly use your free-will against God's natural holy-will for your life?

2. How can you let Jesus use you? (Hint: the aspects to your purpose in life are realized in considering your answer here.)

🙏 Closing Prayer

God, the world wants me to reflect on finding my purpose through self-exploration. The 'me-world' is running a ploy to have me focus more on me and what I can take from this life. Life with you, God, is not completely about me. My purpose is more about finding the crevices of the world where you need me and where you can use me. You gave me my free-will to choose you. I do choose you, God. I want you to show me your holy-will for my life and how I can be used by you to help others. Above all, I want to glorify you, God, in all that I do. Blessed be your name, God. Amen.

For further reading, feast on 1 Corinthians 12:4-11

CHAPTER SEVEN

Able to Harbor No Bitterness, No Resentment, & No Negativity

The Lord is close to the brokenhearted, saves those whose spirit is crushed. Many are the troubles of the righteous, but the Lord delivers him from them all.

† Psalm 34:19-20

As told by Gail:

By the time I reached ten years of age, I had lost two siblings to death. They were the siblings closest in birth order to me. By the time I was raising Alli with her disabilities, I also lost another sibling. I watched as my parents buried three children. Korrine has shared that she feels her upbringing molded her. I also feel events that happened to my family as I was growing up and the reactions of my parents to those tragic events molded me. They helped me decide to never hold on to bitterness, resentment, anger, or anything negative. I learned that it only hurts the person holding onto the toxic feelings.

My parents were Buddy and Fannie Frick. They had eight children given to them, but unfortunately not all their children followed the natural law of order in living past their parents' deaths. They buried three children in their lifetime when their children were twenty-one-months old, fourteen-years-old, and twenty-eight years old. The age of a child at death is a moot factor. The grief is always a consuming and heavy toil to carry and live through no matter the age of the child.

Their children, in birth order, were Antoinette (Toni), Cindy, Buddy (little Buddy), me (Gail), Kathy, Greg, Tina, and Mary. I found myself uniquely between two siblings, Kathy, and little Buddy, who would become angels too soon in life.

I was five years old when the sibling born after me, Kathy, died as a toddler from pneumonia complications. I can remember Kathy in life as my little sibling and in her untimely death. Four years after Kathy died, my family was stricken with another loss. This time it was the sibling ahead of me in birth order, my older brother, little Buddy. He was a young teenager in his 8th grade year of school, and he died of kidney failure. I was only nine years old when little Buddy died. Before the age of ten, I endured losing two siblings, and they were the two siblings closest in age to me.

I witnessed the realest forms of physical pain in illnesses to the point of death in my loved ones. I also witnessed the emotional pain that comes from mourning so deeply. I know the saints bask in sorrow for the closeness they can feel to Christ in those dark times. I can't say my parents basked in the sorrow, but I do know they would not have lived through the tragic losses if not for their faith in God. The realities are that despite grave and dark times, our faith in Christ prevailed.

My parents not only had to bury two children, but they also had to carry on with life for the rest of their children. It is harrowing enough to lose a child, much less two children within a span of four years. The repercussions of these extreme sorrows cast over our entire family.

Faith kept my parents holding us all together. They couldn't be defeated in life, but the sorrows were heavy burdens to carry. Even with a strong faith, my father (for good reason) wrestled with the concept of why bad things happen to good people. Likewise, my mother wrestled with it, but the heavy burdens perhaps weighed her down at times from fully living her life. Mom had a great relationship with the Blessed

Virgin Mary. Mom knew to turn to Mary because Mary of all people could understand the deep sorrow of losing a child, and so the bond between mothers was cemented.

If not for faith to see us through, it could have been debilitating to all of us in the sense that my parents could possibly have lost their mind, lost their body, or lost their soul. Debilitation from a traumatic event can originate from the anger over losing two young lives, which could possibly lead to a life of bitterness and resentment. My parents' faith made the scars of losing two children livable. The traumatic events were scars, but scars can be a beautiful thing when carried in the light of Christ for others to witness. This is what my family chose. They chose their faith; they chose Christ; they chose the light.

Time passed and my siblings and I grew into adults and started lives of our own. As grandchildren eventually arrived, my parents were especially present in our lives when Alli came into the picture. It allowed mom and dad to be needed and to have additional purposes. They could help Terry and me with tangible things as well as through their devoted prayers.

My dad, affectionately known as Grandpa Frick, wanted nothing more than to see my daughter Alli have the use of her arms and hands to feed herself. He made it his mission to also see that Alli knew her purpose and her value in life. Even right up to his death, he worked on his mission and goals with Alli. There was a time during Alli's teenage years when she was extra angered at her life and at her disabled body, and Grandpa Frick knew it. He understood Alli. Understanding someone is one of the best ways to show love. Grandpa Buddy Frick would say he depended on Alli's wheelchair to get him in and out of church. He needed her to bring him to mass. His tested faith over the years of grief reaped him a wise and compassionate heart in loving Alli exactly how she needed loved. God bonded them.

My parents faced another unexpected death of a child while I was busy raising our three school-aged daughters. This time it was the death of an adult child, and it completely rocked our growing extended family.

It was the death of my youngest sibling, Mary. After Kathy and little Buddy had died, Mary was the child gifted to my parents. Mary's birth was a symbol of hope for my family after two children had died.

Mary died shortly after she was married. She was twenty-eight years old the summer of her beautiful wedding. Our entire family, which included grandchildren at this time, had a happy celebration in seeing our beloved Mary happily married. Sadly, just shy of four months to the day after her wedding, Mary died unexpectedly. It was a devastating and confusing thing to understand. Mary suffered a pulmonary embolism.

Why did this have to happen? Why did a recently married, beautiful young woman have to be stripped from this life? Why was she taken away from the ones who loved her so much? My parents already faced so much loss in life with little Buddy and Kathy. It hurt inexplicably deep. Our Frick family had grown so much bigger with so many more hearts broken over losing Mary.

My dad continued wrestling and wondering why good people suffer. Why do good people have to suffer such bad blows in life? He sought answers from his priest at the time. Mom sought answers in her rosary and her devoted prayer life, especially with the Blessed Virgin Mary. It feels like their human capacity to bear such tremendous pain was put to the maximum test. The burdens were heavy. At times the grief felt so heavy it probably hindered them from even feeling alive at times. There is no judgment in how a human handles such devastations as what my parents had. The overall theme linking all their years, including through suffering their losses, was that their faith was firmly planted in God.

I watched them, though. I learned from them. I had no way of foretelling my life would encompass tumultuous times. When those rocky moments arrived for me, I decided I didn't want to carry heavy resentment with me. I wanted to forgive and forget. To me, it means to really and truly let the bad things go. No matter how bad things got, I was and am firm in these convictions. I knew if I held on to resentment, bitterness, and all the anger that comes when bad things happen in life, that those ill feelings would consume my soul and yield me unable to live life and care for my own family. I just wouldn't allow it.

These beliefs carried me through the traumatic birthing event with Alli. I choose only to see the blessings that have arisen from it, such as viewing it as a miracle I survived and that we have Alli alive with us. My resolute faith also has carried me through my marriage, and it has carried me through all of Korrine's MS struggles.

My daughters are not without their own sorrows. In a one year's span of time, they lost both of their grandfathers, who were important paternal figures in their lives, in addition to losing Barry. Barry was another paternal figure in Alli's life that she bonded with at the Jackson Center. My daughters have also lost both of their grandmothers. In addition, there is the mourning the loss of function of their bodies due to cerebral palsy and multiple sclerosis. Sorrow can be an easy instigator to bitterness, anger, and negativity, but these feelings have no lasting place in our fruitful lives.

Some people have told me it is justifiable to be angry with things that have happened in my life. Whether negative feelings are justifiable, I resolved to believe it doesn't make my life any better to hold on to the negative feelings. I know it hurt my parents while they wrestled with the *why* questions, so I try not to allow myself to do it.

When opposition or any form of negativity confronts us, we try to turn the cheek like Jesus tells us to do. We let the negativity go, and then we pick ourselves up and move forward. We never would have found the blessings in our lives had we welled up with anger, bitterness, and resentment. I am very aware of how many positive things have come into our lives. I battle the negative feelings with immense gratitude and acceptance.

God's hands have a way of molding, teaching, and equipping us through others to deal with life's events. I learned from my parent's lives about dealing with tragedy. I haven't directly emulated my parent's actions and opinions, but I chose to foster their steadfast faith. I knew my daughters needed an example to lean on and learn from. How I was shaped and formed in my early life directly reflects the stability and positive force I want to be for my family.

In the Bible in Galatians 6:14 says, "But may I never boast except in the cross of our Lord Jesus Christ, through which the world has been crucified to me, and I to the world." My parents lived this verse through the many sorrows they endured in life. They had a lot of crosses to carry, and a lot of loss endured, which brought them to the foot of the cross daily.

Korrine likes to reflect, and she realizes she is standing on the faith of generations before her. Korrine has described two parables from her heart. She notes the below:

Life can be described in two parables. First, think of the shape of the circle as it relates to the life cycle. We come into this world requiring tedious and continual care and then if you get the opportunity to live a full life you will probably require a lot of help as you leave this life. The good you put into this world will hopefully be returned to you, but likewise, the ill you put forth into this life may present itself in a less than desirable manner as you are leaving this life.

Second, life is like a ship. You build your ship - your life. You get your supplies and you decide what materials to make your ship out of while also discerning your crew and the people you surround yourself with. When it comes time to sail with this ship, this life you've built, you cannot control the currents, the wind, or the weather. You must just sail with it and take what it gives you and make the best of it. You have the choice to put your sail up all the way and go fast and reach great destinations, or you have the choice to keep the sail at half mast to play it safe with no risks. The circumstances of sailing and the circumstances of life might take you a little longer to get where you are going, but it is all your choice.

Life is full of decisions and everyone is different — but the key is to keep Christ involved in your decisions to ensure a safe harbor.

The saints are people to draw inspiration from. They show us how to turn bad things into the good fruits God intends. Author Helene Mongin's book, "The Extraordinary Parents of Saint Therese of Lisieux," gives a personal and in depth look at how Saints Louis and Zelie Martin raised their daughters, including their daughter, Therese, who became a saint before they, the parents, became saints. Helen Mongin shares about the Martin family, who suffered so much, just like our family has:

"Their philosophy of life reflected these trials: 'So, you see, the happiest people are only the least unhappy. The wisest thing, the simplest thing, in all this is to resign oneself to God's will and to prepare ahead of time to carry one's cross as bravely as possible.' This is the realism of a woman whose experience had not made her bitter but had led her to focus on the essential. Their sorrow didn't make them insensitive to the pain of others, it quickened their compassion."

There is no place for resentment, bitterness, and anger in our lives. No matter how turbulent our life gets, we still have a choice. Choose to forgive and forget. God can wash over the negativity. It is wasted time to live in anger, and it is simply not worth.

Prayer for Serenity

God, grant me serenity to accept the things I cannot change,
courage to change the things I can
and wisdom to know the difference.
Living one day at a time,
enjoying one moment at a time,
accepting hardship as a pathway to peace
taking, as Jesus did
this sinful world as it is,
not as I would have it,
trusting that You will make all things right
if I surrender to Your will,
so that I may be reasonably happy in this life
and supremely happy with You forever in the next.

Reinhold Niebuhr

❓ Reflective Questions

1. Name times in your life that were turbulent and when you wrestled with anger, resentment, and bitterness.

2. Can you choose to forgive and forget; and if not, will you choose to focus on faith to see you through until you can forgive and forget?

🙇 Closing Prayer

God, there are things in this world that make me angry, truly angry. At times, I harbor large resentments and bitterness at the plights I have had and at the plights being dealt to my loved ones. I know you can handle my anger. I am allowed to be angry at you, God, because you will help me release my anger if I but turn it over to you. You can take away and heal my negative thoughts, feelings, and actions. Living life with all these bad feelings will do me no good. I want to forgive and forget. I want released from the bondage of negativity. And, above all, I want to glorify you, God, in all that I do. Blessed be your name, God. Amen.

PART THREE

How do we let God guide our lives?

CHAPTER EIGHT

Able to Grow with Family & Friends

*Your adornment should not be an external one:
braiding the hair, wearing gold jewelry, or
dressing in fine clothes, but rather the hidden
character of the heart, expressed in the
imperishable beauty of a gentle and calm
disposition which is precious in the sight of God.*

† 1 Peter 3:3-4

As told by Korrine:

God has a unique way of directing our lives. He gives us families. We grow. We stumble. We change. We grow together some more. This chapter is going to highlight family and how ours has changed and grown over the years.

God connected the details when Chad and I made a life transition from our home in Pike County Indiana where Chad and I coached and taught for many years, to next door in Dubois County Indiana where Chad became an elementary school principal, and I could teach in the same school building. God's plans do not necessarily have a direct recipe for us to follow with adding inputs, stirring, and seeing results overnight. In this case, it was years in the making. Even after a plan was outlined, it took over a year to mix, come together, and prayerfully unfold the way God intended to share it with us.

There was a period in the fall of 2015 when my mom was dealing with neck pain. Alli's body requires daily help, and my mom is the steadfast source of Alli's assistance. When I was in college, I was able to move back home to help when I could, but when I married and had children of my own, I was not as present. Alli needs help being lifted into and out of her wheelchair and other chairs in the home. She needs to be lifted into the shower and assisted there. And she needs lifted to the bathroom facilities. Alli needs assistance with eating her meals. These are things an able-bodied person takes completely for granted on a daily basis, but as a caregiver, my mom has to be mindful of these activities day in and day out. The caregiver especially needs to be mindful of their own absence or inability to do the tasks. With mom's neck pain and her body needing a pause for healing, she was rendered unable to care for Alli as she always had.

There exists a tremendously important fact needing explained right now. My mom wanted to continue Alli's care, and Alli has always deeply appreciated our mom's love and care, but Alli also genuinely desires to be able to do these tasks for herself independently. Alli does not like interrupting others for them to see to her needs. She regularly delays or holds off requesting to do things like using a restroom or having a snack out of courtesy for those around her who would have to assist her. An instance of this is at nighttime when Alli will utilize the restroom before and after brushing her teeth. She does this double-check so during the overnight hours she does not have to knock on their shared bedroom wall to wake mom for her assistance in the restroom. These are invisible truths of how Alli quietly considers other people before her own basic needs. Alli doesn't want to be a burden.

Despite Alli's wish to care for herself, the reality was that Alli needed help during mom's time to heal. When mom admitted to needing help, Chad and I were at a point where we could rearrange our family's life to help her and Alli. Our Whitehead family, all six of us, moved into the Werne homeplace, a ranch house, in Dubois County to assist Alli with daily life.

Some parents might be averse to having their adult children move home with them, but not my mom. My younger sister Kate would concur. Our mom would have all her children and their families move in with her and enjoy every minute of it! This says a great deal about my mom's large heart and the amount of love she has to give. Our Whitehead clan lived there from the summer of 2015 until Christmas of 2016.

After moving our family in with my parents, Chad and I traveled back to Pike County daily together to continue our teaching jobs while our four boys were introduced at the start of a new school year to their new school district in Dubois County. The boys began a new school year in their respective grade levels of kindergarten for our youngest son Kase, third grade for our Irish twin boys Tate and Rolan, and our oldest son Carter began his new year in the sixth grade. It was a transitional year for all of us.

Within the years leading up to the move to Dubois County, my MS had progressed. I was under the Nashville doctor's care, but I was still waiting on the new MS medicine to be FDA approved. I was using walking sticks to move around, but I had to stop driving all together. When my oldest son was only elementary age, he honestly questioned me with my driving abilities. With one thoughtful comment from him, it resonated. My future concerns on that topic were officially a reality I had to deal with, and it proved to be a hard thing to come to grips with. It meant I felt my own independence falling from my fingertips. I could still teach in the classroom, but my physical body was robbing me of independence. These were fresh wounds I was feeling at the time.

In essence, Alli and I joined together to help each other in more ways than one. We didn't look at each other in our situations and throw our hands up in the air in despair. Instead we looked at each other and we said there is a way through this; we just need to take our time and figure it out. And figure it out we did. To supplement our efforts, mom also was able to hire outside, irregularly timed, help from kind individuals in seeing to some of Alli's daily needs. My mom's sisters also help and support our family tremendously. As a family, we figured out what we could and couldn't do and we made it all work.

In this transitional year, Chad and I looked at the bigger life picture and allowed God to guide us in a thoughtful manner. Our steps included building a home across the field from the Werne homestead and Chad obtaining an administrator position at the elementary school located in proximity. In the long-term this has been confirmed as a logistical, providential blessing in all aspects.

I was there to help mom and Alli when they needed help. And now, mom, Alli, and dad are present nearby to assist our clan when needed with all the boys' activities and schedules. It was and is a very communal and mutual union, and it is how God intended a family to interact and help one another.

Not to be left out is our youngest sister Kate, along with her husband Derek and their two boys, who equally play into this mix of the larger, supportive nucleus of our family. During their early married years, Kate and Derek stepped up as the county coordinators of Special Olympics for several years. They did this for the love of the organization but even more so for their love of Alli. As Kate and Derek's boys have reached school age, their lives have spliced together cohesively with all of us at the same school district.

When you can build a home and you live with a known, long-term physical disability like multiple sclerosis, you plan accommodations to make life more manageable and feasible for the long-term. Chad and I planned and arranged our home to suit the needs of our four, growing, and active boys, as well as the needs of Alli and me. A side effect of building a home laid out for wheelchair accessibility is that it was a plan moldable and suitable to include a large, indoor, open space for our boys' sports. Our home is perfect for us. It is perfect for me to manage our home while in a wheelchair and perfect for a large family of boys to grow in athletically, too.

These are the meaningful layers under the broad and visible surface of our transition. The visible transition from one home to another and from one place of occupation to another is wide and can be subjective through some lenses of perception. Within the change, there can be uneasiness and doubts along the way. That's the case with anything new, because ultimately it is unknown until it is lived through. It was the layers of thoughtful details all oriented and connected with family and support which spur the surface and the big items to ultimately see change.

In our family, we planted our feet firmly in our faith and the importance of family. Thus, we were willing participants in the plans God laid out for us. Currently we are on the other side of what felt like a huge transition and there is comfort, peace, and support. We know we are situated where we are supposed to be in our new home and new jobs.

To say it is lively in our home is an understatement with four growing sons. It is commonplace to find the boys playing their sports whether in fun play or in serious down-to-business, competitive play. Like all sibling dynamics, there are innumerous life lessons to be garnered from one another.

Large families tend to have siblings who naturally gravitate toward one another. Sometimes there exists an amicable attraction and positive charge between certain siblings and other times it simply consists of the opposite charge in a friction of personality. It is human nature, but it is how we handle the emotions we feel from those charges that matter and it is where virtue comes into action.

Among our four boys, two of the boys do have a unique habit of gravitating towards one another. They pair up well to square off in basketball pick-up play. Ordinarily it is a very productive thing to help them both improve on a steeper scale. Siblings mean you have built-in playmates while you are younger. But to me, siblings also mean partners for life - if you survive each other through childhood! What you build in childhood can last a lifetime. This is something I want to impart in my boys' minds. I am speaking from the experience of my own sibling relationships with Kate and Alli. I want to teach virtue to my sons, and they never cease to give me the opportunity for such discussions.

Our Whitehead family has acclimated to our new home and new life, but with growing children there is never a dull moment in parenting. One weekday evening, I was manning the homestead by myself after school with Chad gone at evening meetings with work. My parenting skills were put into overtime.

I heard the mellow drones of my fifth load of laundry tumbled softly in the side room, also affectionately referred to as my office because I spend so much time in there! The heart of our house, the physical center, contains our open kitchen where the dishwasher was running a calming hum, too. These sounds all indicated the evening was well underway with routine and I was keeping up with tasks.

Three of the four boys were home with me, and I had their bellies fed with the first round of their evening eating. My temporarily tidied kitchen would be disturbed later when they all reconvened to eat again like active young boys do. The homework was also getting completed at each son's various pace and timing. I had the latest sport's schedules lying on the island and I planned to outline the new dates on the large wall calendars hanging in the hallway by the pantry. Every evening is typically bustling, but I love the liveliness. My underlying cool temperament serves me well when handling all the irons on the fire in our house. I just focus on what is in front of me and handle one thing at a time.

Who needs clean white socks for gym class tomorrow? Check, they are in the dryer and will be ready by morning. Now, I'm not sure about the home-jersey being in that load!

Who needs a new calculator before next Friday? Check, done. It'll be here in two days. Thank you, UPS.

Who needs a field trip permission slip signed off on? Check, it's on the currently deemed clean section of the countertop along the bar. Just a reminder, the "he" who needs it better get the permission slip packed away before the counter gets dirty again!

And which son left the freezer open? Which son has the busted lip that required the icepack from the said freezer? Oh, wait, someone has a busted lip?!

I'm there. I'm not perfect, but I am PRESENT. I'm trying to be on it and not miss a beat in taking care of all our boys' needs. My mother's instinct is heightened. Is it heightened because of my disabilities, because of my impaired vision and wheelchair use? Is it heightened because I have years of experience in the school system dealing with kids of all ages and personality? Ultimately, I think my motherly instinct is heightened because I love Chad and my sons with all my heart. I cherish that God gave each of them specifically to us. It is that simple. I truly appreciate my vocation of motherhood and I try to never take it for granted. Every need and every virtue needing taught I want to be aware of it in the moment and readily available for each of them.

So back to this mother-of-the-year, winning kind of night I was having — with multi-tasking so many things, I thought I'd give myself a chance to relax for a moment. I grabbed my bottle of water and propped my legs up on the chair next to me at our tall kitchen table. Phew. I could take a load off and exhale deeply. Naturally for any mother, though, reprieve wasn't meant to last for very long.

One of the boys came barreling through the double doors from our basketball court garage and into our home's open living quarters with tears rolling down his hot, red cheeks. From my perch at the high-rise kitchen table, I could witness the entire scene.

"You're the meanest ever! You're just mad at me because I beat you!" He exclaimed as his blonde hair glistened from being matted with sweat. Evidently this was a very intense game of one-on-one basketball with his brother - the brother he naturally gravitated to, for better or worse.

Flailing his arms in the air and storming towards the back bedrooms with exacerbated thuds, it all clued me in that this game did not end well out on the court. The two magnetic boys were bringing their squabble off the court and into our home, which meant I was literally back on my feet with an issue to tackle.

Next, with equally loud vibrations, the basketball-playing partner came following close behind from the garage court. "You big idiot, all you do is travel and throw up floaters to the basket. You were just lucky to beat me with that last floater!"

Before I could blink, their cutting words turned into cutting actions. Clothes hangers, socks, and my folded laundry were being strewn about! My heart sank as any mother's heart does when they see their children squabble. I wheeled myself into the situation. It was obvious the boys couldn't compromise their way out of this apparent situation, and it warranted my careful intervention. My boys and their visible fight were the next task in front of me needing attention at this very moment. My focus was on them.

First, I comforted and calmed the son who came barreling through the door initially. He was the injured soul of the altercation. What had happened was typical sibling rivalry. One brother was beating the other brother in an unexpected manner. The brother being beaten was shocked. He went into defensive mode and berated his brother to compensate his own loss. He chose to cut his brother down and ultimately was mean. This was all from a fast-paced, competitive-natured, setup of a game. These underlying factors made emotions run high. The brother had a weak moment and acted out of impulse instead of thought. Regardless of rationale, the recipient brother was hurt and had run off. I consoled and picked him up, and he went on about his evening after licking his wounds.

I wouldn't have as clear-cut a consolation and encouragement for the brother inflicting the harm. This conversation would require much more of me. I rolled over to find this brother still stewing privately with anger and frustration. I knew he was remorseful of his actions towards his brother. It was obvious by his behavior that he was sorry. I was not about to shame him. My job as his mom was to guide him. I had to get him to understand the lasting effects of his actions. Whether he meant to cause harm or not, he did.

In a calm voice, I shared, "Listen, this must stop. You cannot do this anymore. You can't keep being mean to your brother. You know, Aunt Kate was just here earlier today. When she left, we hugged. Maybe it sounds weird to you, but it is a fact that we didn't use to hug. We didn't use to get along either. We're close now, but it wasn't always like this when we were growing up. I was mean to her." I was open and honest. I admitted my own faults in life to show my son some perspective.

"Really?" my young son sheepishly inquired.

"Yes, and I cannot go back in time and take back all the mean things I have done to her. All I can do now is make up for it and be nice now. You don't want to be forty years old and know you were mean years ago. Do you think I remember what I did to her? I don't remember what I did, but I know I was mean to her because she remembers all the mean things I did. She can tell me what I did. I scarred her. Do you want to be that way to your brother?" I looked directly at my son trying to be extra impactful at this very moment.

Nodding, he showed agreement, so I continued. "Do you want to scar your brother? Do you want to be responsible for making him feel that way? I don't think you want to be that way. I can speak straight from experience you'll regret your mean and impulsive actions. So, you need to change now."

We hugged each other, and my young son walked away with a lot to think about. It would be his choice to be more mindful of his actions going forward. As a parent, all I can do is stick with what I like to call my Ps of parenting: persistence, positivity, patience, and prayer.

For us, too, we have the God-ability and choices within our family structure. Are we interacting with those closest to us in a lasting and loving way, or are we allowing our impulses to dictate mean actions? Let's grow together and choose each other. If we can't get along in our own homes, how can we expect there to be peace in our greater communities? Husbands and wives choose each other, whereas siblings didn't get to pick each other; however, they do have each other for a reason since God has them placed together. When personalities clash the most, patience will make the years under the same roof smoother.

Teaching the virtues, which is a firm desire to do what is good, and teaching how to have a growth mindset, are the best tools for a parent. There are a total of seven virtues: prudence, temperance, justice, fortitude, faith, hope, and charity. Prudence is choosing between right and wrong. Temperance is about self-control and moderation. Justice is the right thing for all people. Fortitude provides the courage to do what is right in hard situations. Faith means we believe in all of God's promises. Hope is the ability to trust in God. Charity is the ability to love God first and thus we will be more apt to serve our neighbor through our love of God. Virtue is a wonderful subject to dive into while parenting with those P's of persistence, positivity, patience, and prayer.

Switching gears, it is time someone who has stayed mostly behind the scenes gets a little light shone upon him — my dad, the patriarch of our family. Dad is also known as Terry Werne. He is a hard nut to explain but aren't we all. Some say the word "fun" is found in dysfunctional, so all families are a little bit dysfunctional and fun. To say that my dad is behind the scenes does not mean he loves our family any less. This would be an easy misjudgment made about my dad and about a lot of people who appear distant but really are not.

In a chapter about choosing family, he needs to try to be explained. There are innumerous books regarding Enneagram tests and love languages. These tools can be quite insightful for some people to understand why they interact the way they do within their own family, but also, they can make us just as aware of why and how our loved ones respond to us. The point is not to break apart and analyze my dad's Enneagram classification and his love language, but rather to explain how he shows his love to us in his own way. We know he cares by what he does.

Admittedly, my dad does not have the patience or acceptance as my mom does from Alli's birth and from my MS diagnosis. He wishes that neither of us were dealt the hand we were dealt. He wants to take our struggles away from us. As our father, it is his innate desire to act as his daughters' protector. With things like CP and MS, dad simply can't protect us. He has no power or control over these medical things. I can see how it would be a very heavy thing for a man to handle it.

God gave my mom to my dad, though, and my mom can speak the truths dad needs to hear. As parents to two adult daughters living with disabilities, my mom directs dad to just help as much as he can but not to provide sympathy. Mom knows that Alli and I do not want sympathy or pity. Rather empathy and support for us, however they can, is what they do for us. Their driving abilities help Alli and me a great deal, too!

Dad simply processes our life events in a more personal and deeply internal manner. Maybe it's not categorized as the healthiest way to go about things, but for him and his personality it is the way he sorts through and manages life. He's always supported mom and us girls, but he couldn't always express it in the way we needed or would have liked for him to express it. No one is at fault for how they process and handle things, especially since they are not harming anyone directly while managing the large, heavy issues at hand. If dad processes things inside, he probably is hurting himself more than anyone else.

When Alli was little, it was dad who predominately drove Alli to and from her early preschool classes. Dad was even president of the Patoka Valley Center, where Alli received her important therapies. Years later, Alli showed how much she loves dad at her graduation ceremony from her Ability Camp in Canada. She chose dad to be the volunteer to whom she demonstrated her new abilities at the group program. Dad willingly and gladly participated. Dad came away from Canada with new thoughts on how he could assist Alli in her independent endeavors.

In dad's innovative personality, he built her a chair ladder, built her raised garden beds, and built a special sandbox under a playset so that Alli could play with Kate and me. These were ways dad provided means of inclusion for Alli by tearing down the wall of exclusion from our daily life. He looked for ways he could physically accommodate Alli into our lives.

A few years after Alli came home from Ability Camp, dad was still being innovative for her. With the help of friends, he engineered a special adaptive device with the lawn mower and Alli's wheelchair, so that Alli could literally mow the yard. She was highlighted in the local paper and in the Exceptional Parent magazine. Many parents remarked how they wished their teenager would be as happy to mow the yard as Alli was! Dad helped her achieve it.

Building things to help Alli was and is still the way dad shows his direct and pure love for us. We didn't always understand this kind of love. It has taken a great deal of time to understand and time to accept and receive this form of love. Dad might be a hard nut, but he is our nut.

When Alli started at the Jackson Center for Conductive Education Therapy in Mooresville, Indiana in 2009, she met a wonderful lady named Judy. Judy helped Alli work through her personal feelings and especially her feelings with dad. Alli learned to write letters to express her thoughts to dad. It was a process that provided Alli with a great deal of peace and acceptance towards understanding dad.

Every single family is unique because we are comprised of unique individuals. Relating to and understanding one another is daunting enough, but when thrown curveballs in life with physical disabilities, it is especially difficult. To reiterate, it takes patience, persistence, positivity, and prayer. Don't give up on your family. We can work through any problem with the Ps.

Life's transitions are opportunities for growth within a family. The summer before entering college I felt this type of growth. I sought something outside of myself during that restless summer after I closed the book on my high school years. I found it in my sisters. Perhaps my ill-behavior towards one younger sister stirred me to find virtuous answers in another sister. The following is an essay I wrote from my heart when I was eighteen. My mom saved this letter for all these years and shared it with Alli and me as we were writing this book. It is a full-circle kind of letter to read now after life has brought us to both living with disabilities.

Summer 1997
To Allison
From Korrine

Being patient and having a good attitude isn't something you think about every day, but for me it is something that crosses my mind now. I never used to have a good attitude and by all means I was never patient, but with a little help from my younger sister I slowly began to realize what having patience and a good attitude really means.

You are probably thinking her 'little' sister, but let me tell you just because she is younger does not mean she is not wiser. Allison has something special. She has a big heart. She wasn't fortunate to be born with good legs and clear speech like most people, but she was born with a heart of pure gold.

When I was little, I was never very patient with her. If I couldn't understand her, I would just simply give up and walk away like it was no big deal. Over time, I soon realized that she needs the same attention, love, and moral support as anyone else. You just have to simply take your time and be very patient. It is not just something that comes over night. You have to work at it just like anything else.

If anyone understands what it is like to have a positive attitude, it is Alli. She faces more challenges every day than most people will probably face in a lifetime. It is not always easy for her to wake up every morning with a smile upon her face, hoping and thinking that maybe today will be the day that she will walk on her own. She keeps that smile upon her face and keeps that attitude shining.

I used to have the worst attitude in the whole world. It was ugly. I was the most pessimistic person. I always thought only the worst in every situation and I would think that things were never going to be okay. I made everything seem worse than it really was.

As I grew older, I wanted to change my ways. I didn't want to be impatient and pessimistic anymore, but I didn't think it was possible to change my ways. This is when I turned and took a good long look at Allison. She does it, I thought. She gets up every morning knowing that she could not walk or talk clearly the day before, but yet she still hopes that today is going to be different.

After a long thought-out summer before my freshman year, I realized that you only have a chance to live once and you have to make the best out of what God gives you. I think that everything that happens; happens for a reason. I think what happened to Allison was a presence from God trying to help remind pessimistic, impatient, selfish people that they really don't have life all that bad. Life is never bad. It is just how you make it out to be. You can take any bad situation and either learn from it or turn it into a good one.

It takes a lot more muscles to smile than it does to frown. It sometimes seems that it is much easier to turn to pessimism than it is to take that bigger step towards optimism, but this is when you fight back the hardest. When you are happy and optimistic again, is when you know you have won.

I no longer feel sorry for Allison, and I don't feel anyone else should either, because she is just like the rest of us except she has a few minor physical setbacks. Let me tell you, she has got the heart to make up for it. You cannot be blessed with everything in life, but she was blessed with the biggest and most important.

I could never repay Allison for the things she has taught me. If there was a way though, the biggest way I could possibly thank her is by giving her the gifts she never received, even if it meant losing mine.

I would give up my legs for her, because in return she gave me the true meaning of life.

Korrine

Wow, well I can no longer give Alli the gift of functioning legs the way eighteen-year-old Korrine felt Alli deserved. Instead of giving her my legs, I can give Alli the realest form of empathy because I understand some of her disability plights now. Family means love and sacrifice. We can choose to love our family regardless of our differences, regardless of our past hurts, regardless of our brokenness, and regardless of the struggles and hurdles that come our way. No family is perfect, but a family that seeks God together can survive the deepest sorrows.

We've mentioned prior author Helene Mongin who wrote the book "The Extraordinary Parents of Saint Therese of Lisieux." The entire book is one eye-opening thought after another to truly encourage faith through learning about Saint Therese of Lisieux and her family. In Helene Mongin's book she summarizes the Martin family who is full of Saints by saying, "The canonization of Louis and Zelie underscores that the family can be a place of love so strong that it testifies to the whole world of God's love and that an ordinary life lived with God can bear extraordinary fruit."

Find the extraordinary fruits in your own families, the fruits God wants for you!

❓ Reflective Questions

1. Have your impulsive actions resulted in meanness to loved ones, and have you ever reconciled yourself to that person/people? (P.S. It's never too late to reconcile.)

2. Of Korrine's P's: persistence, patience, positivity, and prayer, which "P" do you need to improve on the most and what steps will you take to develop in that area?

🛐 Closing Prayer

Dear God, no family is perfect, but I trust you placed me in this family for a reason. Help me to be more patient with the family members who most make my blood boil with frustration. Help me to be persistent in my love for each of them and allow positivity to overflow and connect me to all of the varying ways they need me to show my love to them. They may not express their love and support the same way I do, but I know they are still my family whom I love. And, God, when I am most confused with my family, let my prayers to you be enough to carry me through. I want to glorify you, God, in all that I do. Blessed be your name, God. Amen.

Allison

DAVID PIERINI/THE HERALD

Allison Werne, 17, was not about to let cerebral palsy keep her out of family chores. After two years of longing to do it, the Huntingburg girl now mows the family's front lawn, thanks to the ingenuity of her father, Terry Werne, who affixed caster wheels and two metal rods to a lawn mower and hooked it up to Allison's motorized chair. "She loves swimming and bowling," her father said. "But mowing is her top thing right now."

Family fulfills girl's yen to mow

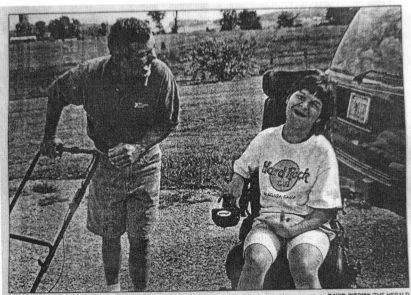

DAVID PIERINI/THE HERALD

Terry Werne usually just starts the mower and lets Allison go until the mower runs out of gas or her chair runs out of power.

CHAPTER NINE

Able to Have Faith

*Jesus said to them in reply, "Have faith in God.
Amen, I say to you, whoever says to this mountain,
'Be lifted up and thrown into the sea,' and does not
doubt in his heart but believes that what he says
will happen, it shall be done for him. Therefore I
tell you, all that you ask for in prayer, believe that
you will receive it and it shall be yours. When you
stand to pray, forgive anyone against who you have
a grievance, so that your heavenly Father may in
turn forgive you your transgressions."*

† **Mark 11: 22-26**

As told by Gail:

Faith is subjectively personal, and yet it is also universal in encompassing and uniting all of us. Faith described this way proves God's omnipotence and sovereignty. Regardless of our denomination of Christian faith, God receives our praise and devotion. Wherever we are in our faith journey, we all have something to gain from being open to hear someone else's witness to their faith in God. It is hard to pluck just one chunk or one aspect of someone's faith to illustrate a formidable witness to Christ, but God touched me in this particular "plucked story" of my faith journey.

I was actually in death's grasp during Alli's traumatic birth in 1981, so it is presumable to think I would have potentially experienced a come-to-Jesus moment while being in the throes of the twenty minute resuscitation. But I did not. I did not see Jesus, angels, or anything supernatural. It was simply a period comprising darkness. I was rather indifferent to it needing to be anything other than what it was, and I moved forward with life.

Fortunate enough, God granted me a different occasion to rely on and experience Him. Through this special occasion, I feel blessed with a second shot at life. It means I was really and truly able to feel God's saving grace. This incident occurred during a family vacation in the mid 1990s.

All three of our daughters, who were school age, were along for this memorable trip, in addition to other friends and family members. Our group vacation trip took us to the state of Missouri, just a couple states away from our home in Indiana, to Hannibal and the historic home place of Mark Twain. The irony is that the town is the setting for *The Adventures of Huckleberry Finn*, and evidently, I had an adventure awaiting me, too.

One of the activities on our vacation included everyone loading up to enjoy a day of canoeing. It seemed like a great activity to soak in some beautiful Midwestern sunshine and nature. The combination of the outdoors with physical exertion makes it the perfect outing for our family. The river we were canoeing on was called the Black River, sometimes referred to as the death river. Strangely, nobody in our group was alarmed by the name of the river. We didn't have any reservations about taking our large group floating down the "death river's" waters.

The canoe trip was off to a great beginning, and the impeccable weather further promoted the hopes of the day. Lathering up in sunscreen and divvying up sunglasses, everyone was scurrying around in preparations with bags flying from one person to another. Coolers were situated into canoes while kids and adults were dispersed accordingly. With lifejackets and all our supplies, we felt prepared and comfortable, ready to have some family fun.

Each canoe took their turn in pushing off the river's sandy embankment and into the easy-drifting, clear, blue waters. The river had a calming effect to it with its glistening waters sparkling like diamonds all around us. The picturesque scenes were not at all indicative of dread and death, as the informal name of the river would signify. Seated inside the canoe, we felt a rolling and mellowing smoothness coming from the currents underneath as the canoes sliced the water. Trees and green growth covered the embankments on both sides of the river providing a majestic and untouched feeling. In the open skies above, birds would swoop into distant spots ahead of us in the river. Now and then the birds would successfully arise with a meal in tow. Squirrels ran weightless from one tree limb to another as if they were chasing the canoes down the river's bend. It was a pleasure to behold the nature all around. It was also enjoyable to banter with one another about our canoe navigating capabilities. Some family members were far more experienced at steering their gliding canoes than others, so it was good-humored fun. It was feeling like a great canoe trip thus far.

As the river's currents picked up pace and became choppier, our canoes diverted creating a bit of space between us. This was nothing to be concerned about. We knew to look out for one another and to meet up accordingly at the ending destination, which is why adults and kids were matched appropriately. Teenaged Korrine and some of her friends were positioned in a canoe ahead of the rest of our group. She was out of sight and well on her way to exploring the Black River with her friends.

My brother, Greg, and his wife Charlotte and their son, Hunter, along with Kate were in canoes a good distance behind Korrine and her friends. Then, bringing up the rear of the group and meandering at our own pace, were Alli, Terry, and I. We were simply following the river's sprawl. As all good parents do, our canoe seemed to be the pack mule carrying the most important supplies like keys and wallets. Loaded down, we enjoyed the slower pace of canoeing.

In a bend of the river up ahead, we saw a new group. It was not Korrine or her friends, nor my brother, Greg, or anyone else on vacation with us. This new group felt like they dropped out of the sky's thin air considering we had not seen them at any point along the canoe journey thus far. This new group appeared distressed. It was hard to see that far ahead on the horizon, but the closer we came to the situation we could hear people in the group screaming for help. Knowing something was wrong and not being a family to shy away from helping someone else, we navigated the canoe towards the group in distress. This was before cell phones were commonplace to have in a time of emergency, so there was no thought to call someone for help. There was only time to get to the problem and help however we could.

The distressed group was hunkered down by a very large tree with its strong roots anchored into the river's deep waters. Its tall, mammoth branches overhung the area creating a secluded and private spot in the bend of the tributary. If people weren't crying for help, it would have been a very pretty location to view along our canoe ride. Unfortunately, it proved to be anything but a pleasant location. There were people hanging from the lower branches slouching onto the river. Thus, it certainly seemed like these people needed dire help. They were hanging on for dear life without any visible lifejackets around them.

The front, slanted tip of our canoe was slicing the last bit of waters separating our two canoe groups. My heart was racing in this emergency. Arriving just in time to help was when this distressed group abruptly changed their demeanor from being in harm's way to being the ones doing the harming. They flipped our canoe completely over, emptying everything it carried including Alli, Terry, I and all of our valuable supplies.

In the heat of a traumatic moment, everything happens so fast. Alli was picked up by the brisk pace of the river's currents after plummeting out of the canoe, and she went sailing down the river in her life jacket. Everything was in disarray. Operating on fatherly impulse, Terry went after Alli to save her from floating all alone to ten-buck-two down the river, while I was thrust down deep below the waters of the river.

We were attacked. I was pinned between a rock and tree roots below me and the canoe above me. I was conscious and fully aware that I was under the river's waters in a drowning situation. This wasn't like my dramatic birthing event where everything went dark in my unconsciousness. This time, my mind was awake and racing franticly. How could I get myself out of this predicament? Where did my leg fall into the crevices of this rock to get pinned? Where could I maneuver my leg back out again? And, in my mode of self-preservation, I worried about where Alli was!

I had zero control and zero power to pull my leg out from the rock. Feeling like I was drowning, I was working with all my might and strength. *This is it*, I said to God. I had the very realistic thought I could die right then and there. I had a come-to-Jesus moment while drowning under the "death river's" water in Missouri, which was states away from my home.

Finally, I felt something physically grab my leg. I have no other way to explain this but to say it felt like the hand of God pulling my legs and feet. While the river's waters always felt pristine on the surface, it was very dark beneath the water. I couldn't distinctly see anything. I couldn't see what was lifting me from the snare of death. As soon as I felt the tugging, the touch of the hand on my leg, I was freed and pulled up to the air!

Gasping for air, I swallowed as much sunshine as possible! I was no longer entangled within the cusps of death. Getting my bearings and wits about myself, I looked around to find there was no one around. I couldn't see anyone! Obviously, Terry and Alli were down the river much further. The people who were supposedly in distress were gone, along with all my group's wallets, bags, and coolers. I didn't see anyone after being tipped out of my canoe and pinned, but I know I was saved by a power greater than myself. I give credit to the hands of God, and I viewed this as my second chance at life. I very easily could have drowned by being pinned under the waters, but I realize there was a reason I didn't die, just like there was a reason I didn't die during Alli's birth. From this, I felt God's presence in a magnified and elevated way. My faith became ever more paramount in my life.

In a unique twist, Greg and Charlotte saw Terry's pipe floating down the river near them. Greg determined that this pipe was a clue something was wrong behind them because Terry wouldn't lose his pipe on purpose. Kate, though a young grade school student herself, could concur with her uncle on the fact her dad's pipe was of value to him. They steered their canoes to tread backwards to see what was going on. They located Terry, who had Alli with him, and together they all found me under those secluded, lurching branches in the bend of the river.

I know my face was in a state of pure shock when they found me. We took the time to mend what we could out of the situation. Sitting along the edge of the river, I assessed myself with the aid of the family. I had a bloody gash and injury on my upper thigh from where my leg had been wedged in the rock. My lungs were strained from the trauma, but I didn't feel short of breath to indicate fluid on my lungs from nearly drowning. I was so glad to see Terry and Alli alive and doing fine.

Our group was down a canoe so together we limped our way through the remainder of the trip to our destination where Korrine and her friends were anxiously awaiting. After rehashing everything to get Korrine caught up on events, we decided we were homeward bound. Being a registered nurse, I stopped at a store to buy steri-strips and fix my leg. My large gash was rough and dirty, so it needed to be cleaned. I might have nerves of steel, but I also made sure to get a tetanus shot when we were home again!

Homeward bound looked different than we thought it would. We had lost our supplies and our important wallets. It's funny the things you recall in the memories of your life. The impact of being scammed and robbed on a canoe trip and the tangible consequences of not having a wallet are moot in the grand scheme. The impact I have from this trip was from being saved when I felt death's grasp while drowning.

There are always people in the world who make bad choices, like those individuals who faked a distressing situation along the 'black death' river. They crossed paths with us and hurt us. I have no recollection of their faces, and nobody has any idea where they vanished to. In the end, the negativity of this random group of people doesn't matter. This event, though, was a prominent component of my life-long faith journey.

I never questioned God about the events that filled my life until one day I was given the chance to explore such a thought on faith. Fast forward a couple decades since the canoe trip and I have three adult daughters and six grandsons, all who are living active lives among the local community. Eyes of the people in public suddenly were awakening to the idea that one family was impacted with disabilities in more than one form. People realized Alli and Korrine were sisters who both used wheelchairs. When in public, people tend to gawk and stare at such a sight. It is an act of harmless ignorance on the surface. If we don't use a wheelchair, we don't fully understand, and inevitably we tend to label it as something negative. Therefore, if two sisters are using wheelchairs, it is misunderstood and felt uneasy and uncertain about.

One Sunday morning, congregation members began to disperse after weekend mass. I maneuvered about tidying the stately, wooden pew we had used for the last hour at mass, and I patiently waited. Life with a wheelchair in your family usually inclines you to allow the crowd to go before yourself due to the task of maneuvering. Alli and Korrine both exchanged pleasantries with our parish family as parishioners walked past us heading towards the heavy exit doors. The rest of our family members were meandering about in a casual manner, also patiently and respectfully waiting.

The morning sun was rising and creating luminous reflections from the colorful, ornately stained-glass windows on the church walls. Our Werne and Frick ancestors form a long line of tradition comprising this parish family. The church structure is a beautiful and historic place in which we are proud to provide God in our praise and worship. The church tradition, the church structure, and the ancestral lines of the parish families all provide a grounded foundation of colossal faith. Grounded faith is a beautiful thing to weather time and strife.

In our wait to depart church on this morning, a beloved and trusted deacon approached me with a bright light in his eyes. Something had obviously clicked for the deacon. He finally realized that, despite Korrine and Alli having different last names, sitting before him were two sisters who were both in wheelchairs.

The deacon shrugged his shoulders and exhaled a huge puff. He looked at me and said, "Gail, do you ever look up at God and say, 'that's enough'?"

I froze in place. I know my forehead scrunched. Hmm. I paused before I gently shook my head. Finally, I responded to the deacon in a lightly confused tone, "Can I do that? Can I say that?"

Up to this point, I never questioned my faith, or moreover, I never had the audacity to question God on the events of my life. Because I chose to see the graces of God, I have always rejoiced in my faith with firmness of heart. I have suffered, but in the unknowns God provided. I still have unknowns — unknowns will always be present. Part of the words we sing at Eucharistic exposition and benediction state *"Faith will tell us Christ is present when our human senses fail."* Few things can feel more warmly enveloping than to meditate on those words. Stable faith never permitted my mind to question God amid my earthly circumstances.

Onlookers see me as the mother who has two of her three adult daughters living with physical disabilities. If I catch your attention for this reason, I would like to share my faith in God more with you so that you can know God more, too. Few people know I was a ten-year-old girl who had lost her two closest siblings. Few know the miracle it is for me to have survived Alli's birth. Few know I felt the hands of God save me from drowning along the "death river." But even more so, few people know the daily blessings I find from God amidst this very full life. God's providence and His presence in my life are what I want to share with others. It may not seem to those who are looking in on us from the outside that our prayers are answered. But they are. All these earthly circumstances strengthened my faith. Ultimately, my daughters and I just want to see the face of God. This is our faith.

If you have trouble with prayer, listen to St. Paul VI words of advice, *"If you have lost the taste for prayer, you will regain the desire for it by returning humbly to its practice."* We have the freedom to choose and the God-ability to practice our faith. God can slap us upside the head with sign after sign and we will never be wiser to it without building our own relationship with Him. It's like any relationship, it is communal and mutual. God desires us. He loves us and wants us near Him. Our love for God never stops growing either. We were made to know God, to love God, and to serve God.

Whatever state we are in with our faith, please read this excerpt and be rejuvenated by it. In Joanna Weaver's book *Having a Mary Heart in a Martha World,* she poses A Test of Love.

St. Augustine once preached a sermon in which he
proposed a kind of self-test to see if we truly love God:

Suppose God proposed to you a deal and said,
"I will give you anything you want. You can possess
the whole world. Nothing will be impossible for
you... Nothing will be a sin, nothing forbidden.
You will never die, never have pain, never have
anything you do not want and always have
anything you do want — except for just one thing:
you will never see my face."

Augustine closed with a question:

Did a chill rise in your hearts, when you
heard the words, "you will never see my face"?
That chill is the most precious thing in you;
that is the pure love of God.

Take the chill that just rose in your heart after reading the above —
which is the pure love of God and choose your faith. Love God more,
love your neighbor more, and in doing so you will love yourself more.

Remember, *"Faith will tell us Christ is present, when our human
senses fail..."* Adore the fact that no matter how disarrayed we become
in the daily grind of life, that we can rest in the fact Christ is always
present with us.

❷ Reflective Questions

1. What events in your life have you felt the hand of God?

2. If you have been stalled in your faith in any capacity,
    what will you do now to show God your pure love for Him?
    How can you Know Him, Love Him, and Serve Him more?

☝ Closing Prayer

*God, I am flawed. There have been times in my life where I
have been supremely happy and yet I failed to praise your
name. And, then there have been times in my life where I was
deeply struggling, and I turned and could not find you. I want
to have faith. Help my unbelief. Help me turn my pure love for
you, God, into the rejuvenation I need or the encouragement
I need to grow in my faith and in my relationship with you.
I want you on my heart like a magnet permanently attached.
I want to glorify you, God, in all that I do. Blessed be your
name, God. Amen.*

CHAPTER TEN

Able to Live for Today

"Dare to dream,
For in the daring
There is defiance to then
Live beyond your
Circumstances."

† **Su Williams**

As told by Allison:

Korrine and I are very adventurous and daring ladies. Is this surprising to learn about us? There is no shame in assuming we might not be adventurous based on our physical appearances and knowing we depend on wheelchairs. One of the purposes of our book is to illustrate direct examples of unproven beliefs. This chapter is also for provoking inner reflection to find each of our own fruitful abilities that might be hiding within us.

We love life and we breathe in life. Korrine and Mom have both saved lives on different occasions with the use of CPR, so quite literally they breathe life! A priest who witnessed a teenaged Korrine save the life of a child who was drowning couldn't praise Korrine enough for her mature manner of acting quickly. He recalled Korrine being the right person at the right place and at the right time. Likewise, the gentleman mom saved with CPR would also agree that mom was providentially present to help him. Living in the present is who we are!

For Korrine and me, we turned our disabilities into our God-abilities to find fullness in our days. The irony is not lost that we crave adrenaline-rushing physical activities while simultaneously having physical disabilities. We do not choose to view disabilities as holding us back in life. Instead, our disabilities propel us to give new things a whirl without a second thought to any "what-if" questions about the outcome. We have disabilities pertaining to our bodies. We are not disabled from life! Likewise, you are not disabled from life, either!

Whether you are an introvert and deeply struggle with shyness in stepping up to a new endeavor, or whether you just struggle with reservations about worthiness and merit to be successful at something new, the core of the strife is dealing with a perceived personal weakness. God did not give us a spirit to be timid but to be powerful with His guiding and powerful love, as Timothy in the Bible so eloquently speaks about (2 Timothy 1:7).

Daily, Korrine and I weave our lives around bodies that simply do not act the way we want them to. A perception is that our bodies are weaker, but what exactly is the consensus definition of the word weak? We don't view our bodies with a negative connotation of weak. True, we can't get up and go run a sprint on the school track or play pick-up ball with Korrine and Kate's sons. We've taken the time to cry, and we've taken the time to vent steam of frustrations and bouts of anger with our bodies. However, we will not sit indefinitely in despair and watch life reel by from the sidelines of our own lives. We want to seize any fun we can with the bodies we have.

At the Jackson Center where I do my weekly therapy sessions, I have been adventurous outside of my family unit. I have had opportunities to go ice skating, zip-lining, and rock climbing to name a few out of the adventures. I view these as amazing opportunities to relish in what my body can do and not what it supposedly cannot do.

Regularly I get to go horseback riding. It's through these occasions I will encourage other individuals coping with a disability to keep trying with their horse and not be scared away after a failed attempt. I speak from years of experience from striving in my physical endeavors.

In addition, one of my favorite sports is swimming because I like to be challenged. I deal with spasticity, making me burn more energy than the average person does daily. My CP challenges and makes it harder for my brain to make my body move the ways I desire. And, I truly have an inability to scream for help in an unsteady moment; yet I want to challenge myself physically with swimming! I do this because I want to live my life to the fullest! Fear has its place in life for good measure to keep us in check and alive, but fear that is full of self-inhibitions does not have a place in holding me and Korrine back from using our God-given body in physical adventures.

One way our family lives fully in the present moment is by simply enjoying each other's company, especially on vacation and recreational activities together. The key to managing things, like our disabilities, is in doing things together. We must support one another, or nobody gets anywhere productively. The day to day living with physical disabilities means the men in our lives like Dad, Chad, Derek, and the six grandsons all work collaboratively to get us around at times. On vacation when we are in the crowded public places away from the identified comforts of home, it is not uncommon for Kate's husband, Derek, and Korrine's husband, Chad, to intercede and literally take charge of maneuvering crowds with Korrine and me in their arms or on their backs. This is part of life for us, and they don't think twice about helping.

In recent years on a weekend boat outing, I took hold of an opportunity for fun and adventure on the lake. I chose to go tubing behind the speedboat my family was using. I liked tubing as a child, and I figured tubing as an adult would be just as fun. My family did the necessary protocols of placing me in a lifejacket and securing me to the floating, circular tube. My spasticity means I can grip a rope tightly enough while going fast on the waters behind the boat; however, my grip is so tight that I also cannot release my hand from the rope very readily. My CP means my brain will not signal to release my grip despite my wanting to release. This was all taken into consideration by my loving family.

I was in position as they started moving on the waters of the lake. I could feel the wind blowing in my face as the boat picked up speed slowly and steadily. The afternoon, summer sun was warming my legs stretched out on top of the buzzing tube. The waters of the lake were smooth and relaxing. I felt bliss in the moments while tubing. Bliss equates to joy — and it was indeed the purest form of joy. My adventurous spirit inclined me to be daring that day, and it yielded the fruits of feeling alive in the moment — and the moments to follow!

The smooth waters turned rough and slashed about. This accidentally flipped my tube over in the water. Because I couldn't release the rope from my hand's tight grip, I became entrapped under the water immediately. I was pinned and could not help myself in this situation. Kate's husband, Derek, quickly jumped out of the boat and into the lake. He immediately swam to my rescue and saved me from the potential drowning situation.

Moments later when finally resting on the boat's bow, I took some moments to calm down. The distressing situation left me a bit frazzled. I soon realized I had lived through it, and ultimately, I lived in the moment! It was enjoyment on the tubing jaunt, and the crisis was minor! After tubing, I further lived in the moment by enjoying one, and only one, of Kate's "special" drinks. I wouldn't have any of these memories if I allowed my disabilities or my inhibitions to stop me from living life. What bothers me in life is when I see able-bodied people not taking care of their bodies or not using them. I hope you'll take a moment to think of ways to use your body for the good!

As told by Korrine:

Sisters are like one another, and Alli and I maintain this claim. An example of how I chose to live in the moment, like Alli did with tubing, was when I responded to a daring escapade during a different family summer vacation in 2017.

This family vacation was set on the beach. Having just enjoyed an enjoyable supper together at a restaurant, our family was meandering about a strip of sights and spectacles located near the hotel as the evening was fading into dusk. The fun activities and attractions were proving to be a perfect conclusion to our day. At this time, my MS had me utilizing a wheelchair to move around, but that didn't stop me from wheeling right up to the maze of metal spindled queues at the entrance of a free fall event. The most daring ride on this strip of activities appeared to be the free fall event, and this is what I was attracted to and determined to do!

My initial attempts were futile in trying to coax Chad into doing the free fall with me, because Chad prefers to keep his feet planted on the ground and not go skydiving. "I only want to be flying in the air to dunk a basketball," Chad teased me. I respected my husband's wishes, so I moved on to acquire who I thought would be the perfect person to free fall with me — my youngest sister, Kate.

Chad looked at Kate and basically said if she didn't do it, he would. Further compiling validity to my proposal was Kate's husband, Derek. He used his genius math and engineering skills, analyzed the ropes and their configurations as to the efficacy of our fates on the ride before he confirmed no objections were coming from him. Let's just say Kate was basically compliant and indifferent to my wishes, but she was not as eager and zealous as me about a free fall.

This vacation atmosphere had lights flashing high above us in the dark sky. It was as if the exhilarating lights were urging us to explore life. Looking up and down the strip, we could see faces with laughter and merriment radiating from groups gathered at all the attractions. This was a vacation haven here on the strip. People came to take a reprieve from their normal lives. They were seeking joy found in new things and new sights.

Kate and I looked at our six sons interspersed among our large family. Then, turning the opposite direction of our loved ones' faces, we took a long, discerning glance at the boom which was constructing the free fall event. Lastly, we simply looked at each other and committed to do it. We wanted to chase the adrenaline rush. We wanted to live life on this day! Regardless of how fearful Kate was of the free-falling idea, she wanted to do this to support me and to live her life in a brave way, too. We were on vacation and seeking some joy in this new thing!

Handing our personal jewelry and purses to the boys on the sideline, we bravely strutted away from the safe zone of family and onward to tackle the ride. We boldly tackled what the rest of the family perceived as an audacious challenge. "This is going to be so cool, Kate. Just wait and see. You will be so happy after we do this!" With such positive persuasion from me, how could Kate not be confident to do it?

The metal spindled queues felt like an imprisonment for Kate during our duration in line. Both of our hearts were pounding as we inched forward through each nook and cranny of the queue, but for different reasons. Kate's heart thumped briskly from trepidations and my heart thumped from the happy anticipation.

Realities settled upon us once we arrived at the front of the line. The workers were upbeat and friendly as they greeted and accommodated me while pushing my wheelchair to the side cubby. I could bear my own weight, so I qualified to do this ride. Alli would have liked to attempt such a ride, but she could not fully bear her own weight as required for this free fall event. Thus, this was more motivation for able-bodied Kate to conquer her fear and do this for both Alli and me.

The instructors were providing guidance on how the free fall would work. Not intending to discount our guides' directions, Kate was too enraptured with the view to pay any attention to them. She couldn't shake the anxiety she already felt from where we were perched. Kate was alarmed at the impending view she would have from ten stories higher.

"Kate, did you hear them? Can you handle pulling this trigger once we are in position up there? You'll have to pull it, or we'll never disengage to free-fall." Despite my attempts to alert Kate, she continued to be in a trance or a daze of some sort.

Kate was scanning the crowd, and she thought she could spot her boys, Wyatt, and Webb, standing next to her husband, Derek. Surely Wyatt and Webb would think their mom is like a superwoman flying in the sky like this. She told herself that her boys would think she was cool and amazing, so of course she could handle it. She could handle anything for them. Yet, hesitations were building, and Kate thought about whether the cords tethering them would break just as we were doing the free-falling.

I could see the worry and anxiety filling Kate's face, so I jolted her back to reality by firmly patting her shoulder. "Kate, are you ok? You got this. Right?" With a stern look, Kate gave me the eye of agreement, or the eye of the tiger, signifying she understood.

The guide interrupted us. "I'll need to get you each harnessed in here securely." She motioned us to get situated at the base of the equipment. Kate felt completely unsafe lying face down towards the concrete. Kate thought there was going to be more than the flimsy ropes to protect her. I figured the instructors knew what they were doing so I remained cool and casual as we were latched into place. Kate's thoughts were written across her face: *What on earth did Korrine get me into? Is it too late to say anything now?* I could see Kate become frozen and unable to speak up.

From out in the crowd, looking up at us, our family said it looked like everything was going smoothly. The overhead twinkling lights illuminated their view to see us getting harnessed into the gear and ascending to the summit. Alli had her smartphone in place and ready to take pictures of the grand adventure we were undertaking. Alli was happy for us and glad I had convinced Kate to do this! Derek likewise was ready with his smartphone to record this possible once in a lifetime feat of his wife's.

Reaching the crest of the free fall mechanism, I soaked up the air that somehow felt cooler and more refreshing up there high in the night sky. The warmth from the day's sunshine had penetrated the strip's surface to emit heat into the evening hours, so the sky seemed so much purer and gentler from this elevated vantage point. Lying parallel to Kate, we were facing the cement ground which was now ten stories horizontally below us. This free fall would feel like the direct opposite of a resting yard hammock. Instead of providing a safe cocoon a few feet above the ground like a hammock, this free fall was a gravity-defying, pulling harness on your body. The free fall allowed you to see your fate below you in a non-relaxing, non-hammock manner. Kate felt the unease of staring at the canvas below her, but for me it was life-breathing. I felt invigorated and alive in this swaying state above the crowd. Adrenaline pulsed through my veins with excitement, whereas adrenaline pulsed in Kate's veins with apprehension.

"It's time, Kate. Let's do a countdown and then you can pull the trigger on three, ok?" I took a long pause to soak up the last moments from our height and then I proceeded. "Three, two, one, go!!!!" My voice echoed in the sky, but evidently my tones were falling on deaf ears with Kate, because we went nowhere. There we were. We were just dangling high in the sky with the concrete ground below us. Inaction and an eerie nothingness resounded in a way those standing below could understand. Something wasn't right. We weren't moving.

Kate couldn't hold her fears in any longer. Her alarmed soul signaled tears forming as the waterworks overflowed from her fear-filled eyes. Crap! Was the first word I really thought to myself of the predicament in the moment! Kate was nearing hysterics, so I started reeling off every word of wisdom I could muster. My calm words were not soothing Kate, who was now shaking in her harness. Why did Kate have to be the one controlling the trigger? Why didn't the guide put me by the trigger instead? It was too late for me to answer the questions churning in my head; I had to think forward not backward.

"Come on, Kate. I'm begging you to pull the cord. Will you stop crying? Look, we are going to be fine. I can't enjoy this anymore if you are going to be so upset about it all." My rational comments finally turned into authoritative gestures when I quipped, "Listen, Kate, the sooner you pull the dang cord the sooner this will be all over!" Sisterly love comes in all forms, including tough love when needed like this exact occasion!

Unexpectedly, Kate finally and unmistakably pulled the trigger! We went airborne! The flying was a pendulum motion, swinging us in the vast air, back and forth with no respite or pause. We were soaring and swaying within the ten stories worth of enormous space. We knew our family members were in the vicinity, but there was no way to decipher such details while in motion. Kate's sobbing didn't cease, but it was at least waning thanks to the fast motions of the free fall. This was like nothing we had ever experienced before. It was almost as though we were eagles swooping into a river and then spring-boarding back into the high skies again. Completing the ride, Kate was ever so happy to be back on solid ground and out of the confines of the harness. I was just glad nobody had peed their pants in the process of descending!

In the end, what matters is that we did it and we did it together. Regardless of the little memories making it feel less than ideal, like Kate's crying, we did it. Kate showed her sons what it means to be brave, which is doing something even though it scares you to do it. I showed my sons what it truly means to live life to the fullest no matter your circumstances and disabilities. I wanted to show them with sheer example I would not let a physical disability stop me.

Rest assured, we are not advocating you go tubing in a lake like Alli or fly like a bird in the sky like Kate and I, nor do we encourage any form of dangerous activity. We're simply advocating that you don't let life pass you by.

To some, what brings them life is going on a mission trip with their church group. To others, it is going jeeping on back country roads and soaking in God's views. Yet, to others what breathes life into them, in retirement for instance, is turning their farm into a place for grandkids to raise 4H animals. Hobbies, physical exertion, and nature are wonderful pillars of the things that are out of the ordinary day but can breathe new life into the soul and be rejuvenating. Vacations do that for some people, while others prefer to sit on their porch with time on their hands for quiet reflection to find relaxation. The point is we need to find it. We need to find the things that bring us life because those things also bring us pure forms of happiness.

Often in support groups, like I find with my MS support groups, there are individuals in darker times with their diagnosis. When consumed by disparities, people tend to feel like life is passing them by. I believe it is your choice to not allow life to pass you by. In my daily life, I am admittedly fatigued. My eyes twitch in the cold, and the heat of summer melts my body into a Jell-O form. Yes, I must rely on a wheelchair for mobility. And, yes, due to my impaired vision, I literally have memorized my sons' gaits to figure out where they are amidst the different players at ballgames. I choose to persist through all of this to be present and optimistic for my sons. I persist to be an equal and supportive partner to my husband. I persist through all of this to be a support to kids in the school where I work. And I do all of this because I live the life I have today. Life will not pass me by. With or without a disability, you should not let your life pass you by, either.

God's life within us will be the extent to which we can help others but also the extent to how in tune we are with what God wants for us in this life. Maybe we'll feel the desire to zip line or go tubing like Alli or maybe we will try a free fall event like I did. Life surprises us when we are open to God's plans for our life. Also, doing things for others might possibly breathe the most life into our souls. Volunteering our time, talents, and treasures are certain ways to feel we are living a full life today.

The Benedictines living at the St. Meinrad Abbey in St. Meinrad, Indiana have a prayer book. In it they pray, *"Father, you created me to be Your living temple. I open myself to Your presence. Come and live in me. May Your Holy Spirit, living and working in me, transform me into the likeness of Your beloved Son, Jesus."* If we really struggle in life at figuring out what brings us joy, at what brings us happiness, and at what brings us LIFE, then say this prayer often. Say the words. Reflect on the words. And allow God to show you how to enjoy life. We have a choice.

We can choose to not allow this one life to pass us by. Live it well. Live it with our fruitful God-abilities.

⬛ Reflective Questions

1. What inhibitions, or excuses, do you tell yourself for why you are not living life with sparks of joy and happiness?

2. What inhibitions, or excuses, do you tell yourself for not stepping out of your comfort zone to volunteer and contribute to someone else?

🙇 Closing Prayer

God, I do believe this is a beautiful life. You didn't place me on this earth to not enjoy it. I know I deserve joy and happiness. I am sorry for the times I allow myself to feel disheartened and discouraged by the grim ways the world infiltrates and disturbs my mind and body. I will choose to discover ways that you breathe life into my soul, and I will seize the moments to find my joy and happiness. Joy is a gift from you, and I am to behold it. I want to glorify you, God, in all that I do. Blessed be your name, God. Amen

PART FOUR

Why do we want to help others with physical disabilities?

CHAPTER ELEVEN

Able to Help Others & Use Empathy

But the Lord said to Samuel: Do not judge from his appearance or from his loft stature, because I have rejected him. God does not see as a mortal, who sees the appearance. The Lord looks into the heart.

† 1 Samuel 16:7

As told by Gail:

"Mom, other aisle," Alli speaks up and motions at me as I give her a nod in amicable agreement. Alli remembers where we needed to find the peanut butter and chocolate Nature Valley bars. In thanks, a grin warms upon my face. Alli is a needed companion for me on this grocery trip and any other shopping trip for that matter. Alli helps me more than most people realize and know.

We move onward into the breakfast aisle containing the bars. Children point and try to speak to Seal, Alli's CCI (Canine Companion for Independence dog), but Seal dutifully ignores their pleas and focuses on Alli. This is a natural part of being in public with Seal. He always seems to gain attention. Just like Seal, Alli and I have become immune to gazes and go about our business, too. Our business at the moment was to complete the shopping.

I scan the shelves for the Nature Valley bars, but Alli buzzes by me with Seal by her side. They are headed toward the oatmeal cartons located deeper in the aisle. Alli is very skilled at maneuvering her automated wheelchair without disrupting any products. Controlling her spastic arms, Alli purposefully uses her arm to knock a carton of oatmeal to the ground.

"Seal, get." Alli gives the first command in a series of commands to Seal. He will obediently do each task, one at a time. With the carton of oatmeal in Seal's grasp, Alli provides the next task for him. "Seal, up." Seal takes the oatmeal carton to our grocery cart nearby, props his front paws up on the side of the cart, and patiently waits for his next command from Alli. The next command is to drop it in the cart. Then, Seal is told to get off the cart. "Seal, off." With that final command from Alli, Seal successfully completes loading one of our last items into our cart. Dropping the oatmeal, he only partially sways the grocery cart, this time from left to right, but not bumping anything or anyone. Another achievement for the morning was in the books for the combo of Alli and Seal.

We wrapped up our shopping and headed to the busy checkout area. For some shoppers, we appear like a parade with which to gawk. To impatient shoppers, we are in the way. We have slowly tried to become immune to negativity in public. In trying to ignore stares, people's comments are not as easily ignored sometimes.

Alli moved from our checkout lane towards the front walkway of the store to be out of the way in her wheelchair. I continued to load our groceries and I had my attention steered to the worker. In Alli's absence and approaching me from behind was a familiar acquaintance. She adjusted the scarf around her neck and cleared her throat to get my attention before expressing, "Gail, I just want to tell you how, as for you caring for your daughter, how much we think of that."

I was sucked into a vortex I didn't foresee or desire on a routine shopping trip. My face froze, my hands grew clammy, and with a wounded, racing heart, I felt utterly and completely misunderstood.

Why did this lady, who regularly sees me in public, feel the need to share such a comment? Changing this acquaintance's perception, which was perhaps years in the making, would be much too large a task within the busy checkout line at the store. Rather than implode with every rational and lucid truth pulsing inside my soul, I simply responded, "Alli is a blessing. She's an absolute blessing in my life. I couldn't do my shopping without her."

Finishing my payment and turning the cart to the direction of the exit, Alli and I along with Seal left. Fully capable and independent of one another, Alli and I strolled out of Wal-Mart with our heads held high with dignity. The warm, bright sunshine flooded our faces with comfort and peace, and it became an enveloping feeling lifting us upward to God. Because it was such a pretty day outside, we were not parked up front in a handicapped parking spot as one would assume we would use. Instead, we left the handicapped spots for someone who would need to park closer to the store's entrance more than we did. We would enjoy the sunshine and our beautiful mother-daughter relationship. This was a perplexing and memorable encounter of ignorance while shopping.

Misconception, like this well-meaning lady had, lead to rendering sympathy far too readily to those simply not wanting or needing it. Instead of sympathy, I and my girls could use empathy. We all could use empathetic love. Empathy is the ability to understand what another person is feeling from their vantage point. Too easily, we are quick to form misconceptions of others because we only see certain dimensions and not the whole scope of someone else's life. And, Alli would appreciate interaction with strangers who see her. People in the public often seem to overlook her and focus their attention to Seal or me.

No one escapes life unscathed. How we mold and grow from life's trials, with our faith in God, will generate the kind of empathetic love we give to others. When we live with issues, we don't overlook others anymore. We understand empathy and we give it. Choose to be quicker to smile and understand than to be quick to assume. C. S. Lewis is famous for teaching us that God doesn't play favorites in deciding who gets to understand or see signs from Him more than someone else. Rather, C. S Lewis essentially makes us aware of whom we see in the mirror. If our mirror is dusty, if our relationship with God is dusty, it will be less clear for us to see God and see him in our situations. Conversely, if we can't see God in our circumstances, it will be harder to share His love. The love that every human needs from another human being is compassion and a true empathy, which are sources of God's goodness.

As told by Korrine:

This idea of choosing empathy is exemplified in the tiny societies and communities where children typically are gathered — the school setting. The dynamics between the students are lively and diverse, allowing for ample opportunities to see empathy and positive things.

For any child, the words "I see you" are three of the greatest words an adult can say. They are also three wonderful words to say to any human being. We want to be seen, and we feel seen when shown true empathy. Thinking of every child, giving them everything you have, every day, is a great mission for a great school to illustrate true empathy — but, what does that look like?

One school day, a disagreement amongst a couple of girls developed during lunch dismissal. Breaking a school rule, one little girl jumped on the backside of another. "You are heavy," was quickly stated authoritatively by the girl being jumped on to the little girl doing the jumping. With this choice of words, it completely crushed the heart of the other little girl. Deeply offended, the girl jumped off the backside of the ill-voiced girl, and she sprang into self-defense mode with equally hateful words in return.

I was working as a teacher's aide, and I watched the entire situation unfold from an aisle of lunch tables over. I rolled my push-wheelchair toward them as rapidly as I could. Intervening, I calmed the girls to a quieter level. Once I had their full attention, I shared a quick story with them.

"I'll give you each a tube of toothpaste. You'll each have your own. Can you picture it?"

Confused at first, they responded with, "Yes," and they nodded their heads to indicate they understood and were picturing their toothpaste tubes in their hands.

I continued, "Now take your tubes and squeeze all the toothpaste out and onto the lunch table. Do it. Squeeze it all out. Imagine it."

"Okay, I got a big pile of toothpaste, Mrs. Whitehead. Now what do we do?" One of the little girls chimed in while really getting into the activity.

"Now, you need to put all of the toothpaste you just squeezed out back into your own tube," I said.

Looking at each other, and then returning their glances to me, they sputtered, "But, we can't. We have a big mess, and it can't go back in the tube."

Concluding the parable, I said, "Exactly. You cannot put the toothpaste back in the tube, and it is the same way with your words. You cannot put words back in your mouth after you have said them. You need to filter your words and not say things that hurt others."

Interrupting my lunchroom abruptly was Mr. Whitehead's entry. Routinely, my protocol is to dismiss aisles of children from lunch while reminding them of manners. Manners to say thank you to the lunch ladies and manners to take care of their responsibilities with their trays and with their actions. Being sidetracked by a teaching moment with this group of girls, I was caught off guard to see my tables being dismissed without me.

"No, no, Mr. Whitehead," I spoke up. "This is my job." I wheeled as fast as I could while waving my arms in his direction to stop Mr. Whitehead from interceding in my jurisdiction of the cafeteria at lunch time. Immediately, giggles spread throughout the girls who were listening. They loved it. They love to see Mr. & Mrs. Whitehead working together. The positive, clean banter between their leaders give the students the positive stability they don't even realize they need. Because of the positive and stable environment, the students can then be receptive to the goodness being taught to them in the school community. There is a trust established from this foundation of goodness. This is a concept that furthers the goal of giving every kid everything in every day.

Days are full. Minds are full. Thus, emotions sometimes dictate the words coming out of mouths. Are our words given to one another kind, necessary, or true? Training children to be mindful of the most basic human character trait of kindness is paramount in my purpose and goal of working daily in the school system. It requires loving care in the school to guide the kids on their individual path. It takes true empathetic love. There is no room for sympathy, blame, or shame — only understanding.

Choose empathy and the true love like Christ taught us. Choose helping others. Choose thinking of others. Take heed of Matthew Kelly's power-punching question in his book "Rediscover Jesus" where he asks, "When was the last time someone confused you for Jesus?" Choose the teaching Jesus gave us in His Beatitudes.

The Sermon on the Mount, Beatitudes
Matthew 5: 3-12

"Blessed are the poor in spirit,
for theirs is the kingdom of heaven.
Blessed are they who mourn,
for they will be comforted.
Blessed are the meek,
for they will inherit the land.
Blessed are they who hunger and thirst for righteousness,
for they will be satisfied.
Blessed are they who hunger and thirst for righteousness,
for they will be shown mercy.
Blessed are the clean of heart,
for they will see God.
Blessed are the peacemakers,
for they will be called children of God.
Blessed are they who are persecuted for the sake of
righteousness,
for theirs is the kingdom of heaven.
Blessed are you when they insult you and persecute you and
utter every kind of evil against you (falsely) because of me.
Rejoice and be glad, for your reward will be great in heaven.
Thus they persecuted the prophets who were before you."

❓ Reflective Questions

1. Which Beatitude speaks to your heart the most as you read them?

2. What can you do to be more empathetic and loving to someone you will see tomorrow?

🙏 Closing Prayer

Jesus is the master and teacher. He humbled himself in washing the feet of his apostles and thus showed us the greatest example of how to live. "If you understand this, blessed are you if you DO it." God, help me to turn the love in my heart for you into action. Help me to do what you want me to do in helping someone next to me. Awaken my senses to those around me and the actions I could take. I want to glorify you, God, in all that I do. Blessed be your name, God. Amen

John 13:17 for further reading

CHAPTER TWELVE

Able to Educate and Be Aware – Disability Advocacy

As he passed by he saw a man blind from birth.
His disciples asked him, "Rabbi, who sinned,
this man or his parents that he was born blind?"
Jesus answered, "Neither he nor his parents sinned;
it is so that the works of God might
be made visible through him."

† John 9:1-3

As told by Gail:

Salty, ocean winds wafted through an attendant's daggering words, "I'm sorry sir, but we have a rule of no motorized vehicles or animals on the greens at this golf course."

Befuddled, Terry responded, "But, this is how we always do it. My daughter uses her automated wheelchair and follows my wife and me along the golf course."

"It won't work. No motorized vehicles or animals are allowed," rang the worker's confirming exchange, while simultaneously halting the pleasant, vacationing vibes Terry had felt. "The service dog could sit in the golf cart, if that would help, but he must stay in the cart the whole golfing game."

Feeling deflated, Terry, a proud father of not just one but two adult daughters living with physical disabilities, walked away from an anticipated, relaxing day of golfing while on vacation. Alli felt even more deflated than Terry. Alli felt completely saddened because she didn't want to be the reason Terry and I couldn't enjoy a round of golf. In the same breath, we wouldn't accept Alli not being part of our typical vacation recreation.

Sadly, and perhaps surprisingly, this event transpired the third week of October in 2020, which is modern day America! Disability discrimination, like what was demonstrated at this golf course, still happens frequently in every aspect of life; yet so few understand it unless it directly affects them. Is it a lack of awareness to the concept of physical disability or is it a lack of kindness and empathy to the plight of our fellow mankind? Unquestionably, it is a lack of seeing and choosing the good.

Thinking only in the black and white of rules, the golf course attendant never gave Alli the chance. Like so many, this golf course attendant never recognized Allison's total understanding coming face to face with their lack of awareness and their blunt ignorance. How do we bridge able-bodied citizens to have a more harmonious inclusion with those physically disabled in society? The physically disabled group is the largest minority group that exists, and it is also the minority group any of us could belong to at any given point in our lives!

Statistically, one in four Americans will have a physically disabling event before they reach retirement. There is no guide, no personal advocate, and no angel who will magically come to your aid the minute you reach a disabling aspect of life. Until it affects us, we simply cannot understand the difficult journey of a physically disabled person; however, we can broaden our scope of understanding by thinking outside of ourselves by listening. This is the first step in caring and having an empathetic nature to put goodness into the world. See the good.

This incident at the golf course is not a single instance of adversity our family has faced. Because this is sadly not abnormal, Korrine and

Alli have created presentations they call D.A.B.S. (Disability Awareness by Sisters) to share their witness. Below is essentially a transcription of a talk they gave to young teenagers.

Korrine and Alli talked to teenagers at the St. Mary's Activity Center. This activity center is like any other gathering building sitting alongside a church. It is a building which absolutely comes to life with spiritual formation when filled with its congregants. Stretching out in folding chairs, teenagers take a reprieve from their full week into a reclining state to listen to my girls. The darkness outside creates a serene and calming environment in the otherwise aging, large structure. These teenagers are present for their Wednesday evening religion class at St. Mary's Catholic Church. Alli and Korrine utilize a power point presentation in their talks to groups because Alli's speech is difficult for others to understand. With the power point, people can follow along with the information Alli is sharing with them. Their presentations are very active because they include volunteers to prove their points.

"Now remember, on the count of three, you will take these bags and boxes of groceries from the carpeted floor in the hallway, across these double doors, through this entire length of the cafeteria and then stack them up on that empty table at the far end. Can you handle this?" Korrine is speaking directly to a volunteer from the group of middle school students.

The volunteer, a tall, broad-shouldered, athletic, teenager was very able-bodied and excited to put his muscles to use in front of his peers. Grinning ear to ear, he confidently replicates Korrine's high level of energy, "Yes, I am ready!"

With the iPad in her lap, Alli will be ready to use her head-pointer apparatus to click the start button on her timer as soon as Korrine gives the word to go. This was definitely going to be an opportunity for this teen to strut his stuff in a timed event.

"One, two, three, GO!" Korrine cheers.

The class relatively retains their quiet state as the volunteer does all the work. He provides their entertainment. His agility allows him to handle a lot of items in one swoop of his arms. Maintaining his grip on the cereal boxes and the bags full of heavy canned goods, he races in a straight and direct path down the cafeteria. Then, he heads back across the cafeteria and Alli's iPad shows his very impressive time of twenty-eight seconds for the feat. The report of his time finally elicited some cheers from the students who were otherwise sitting in their seats with a quiet tension from the challenge. They had nothing to compare this demonstration to thus far, so sure they would clap for him. He was out of breath after all the sprinting.

"Very good!" rang Korrine's praises which were now echoing off the cafeteria's tall ceiling.

In her calculated move, Korrine temporarily vanishes through the double doors.

Eyes brighten on the faces of the students in huge speculations to see Korrine now bring an additional push wheelchair to the center of the room. Alli and Korrine are both presenting in their daily wheelchairs, and they brought along a spare one to incorporate into their talk.

"Now, you get to really show us your moves. Hop in this chair. We are going to time you as you bring the groceries from the table where you ran them to a few minutes ago and back to where they originally were through the double doors."

Chuckling to conceal his obvious hesitations and inhibitions about his next task, the volunteer was a good spirit and he bounded into the pushchair and awaited Alli and Korrine's cue to begin his new challenge.

"Alli, are you ready?"

With Seal resting next to her in the most leisure of ways, Alli nodded her head at Korrine.

"One, two, three, go!"

The teen placed his hands at his sides on top of the wheels of his new mobility device. Initially, he went backwards. Then, he somehow slid to the side with the motion of his wheels not being in sync. Finally, after spinning an entire circle, he figured out how his new set of wheels operated. If the prior exercise was entertainment for the class, this was certainly amusement for them. They were not laughing *at him;* they were laughing *with him*!

Now understanding how to move forward, this still did not assure his straight path. The volunteer steered into empty tables and chairs, creating a mess of a bigger obstacle for him to pass through. He'd have to back up, steer to the right, and then back to the left again before surmounting his former clear path. After many attempts and a large lapse of time, he finally crossed the length of the cafeteria. Cheers and applauses of encouragement belted from the onlookers. They wanted him to succeed.

Approaching the table filled with his groceries, he had to get close enough to the table without knocking over the items. It seemed more daunting to him than the parallel parking he was trying to figure out in driver's training! Flank the table; don't knock the table. Sounds easy enough until you are the one controlling the mechanics of the task. And, just like parallel parking, he didn't master it in his futile first attempts. With his extra-long arms, he was able to improvise, grab items, and then set them on his lap. Recognizing he couldn't hold as many items as he did when he first did this exercise while on his own two feet, he committed to only those few items on his lap before attempting the return trip. The debacle continued until the determined volunteer returned most of the groceries to their origin.

Heaving his chest, he was noticeably out of breath from the second challenge by the time he returned to the front of the room. Trying to boost his morale by not reporting an exact time, Korrine merely shared it took him more than five minutes this time to complete the same task, which was a stark contrast to his twenty-eight seconds when he was able bodied.

Continuing demonstrations, instead of popping wheelies or drag-racing their wheelchairs, Alli had a better activity to garner the attention of teenagers — texting!

Korrine asked for a new victim, or volunteer, with a cell phone. All the students' heads flashed to their religion class teacher who was holding a plastic ice cream bucket at the corner of the table. The bucket contained all the students' cell phones brought to class this evening! Religion teachers are the smartest!

The chosen volunteer was handed her personal cell and Korrine explained the new task. "You are going to race Alli in texting me something. Since Alli has spasticity in her arms, how do you think Alli texts?"

Some kids looked downward in a very visible act of being uncomfortable and unsure how to answer. Coming to the aid of their distresses, Korrine continued to explain. "Alli uses a head pointer apparatus to primarily communicate. It simply uses Velcro and attaches to her head securely. The pointer part is like her finger. Alli has a spare head pointer so our volunteer can use one also."

"Are you up for the challenge?" Korrine directed her question to the new volunteer who now had all faces on her and Alli. Sensing the attention, a sheepish grin slowly grew upon her face to indicate she was game.

With a smartphone in the student's hand and a smartphone in Alli's lap, and both ladies equipped with a head pointer, the contestants were ready. "Please text me the following: I love to eat pizza and drink coke. Now!"

In a matter of seconds, Korrine's phone was dinging with a text — from Alli. Eventually Korrine received a second text from the student who was catching up. Eyebrows were rising with surprise. The students were indeed impressed, so several students expressed the desire to challenge Alli. Alli was happy to oblige and ultimately school them with her texting skills in every contest. Each time Alli was able to beat the student in texting with a head pointer. The students were flabbergasted at how fast Alli was.

Turning their concentration to a more sobering demonstration, Korrine flashed an eye chart on the projector screen. Clearly, the student in the back of the room could read most lines of the chart, just like they would at an eye doctor appointment. Korrine had them read a line and very factually the student correctly responded the right items in the line.

The humbling aspect arose for everyone in the room when Korrine flashed the next eye chart on the board. This second chart was completely blurry for everyone in the room. From the person in the front to the person in the back row, all anyone could see were blurry objects in rows on the chart.

"This. This right here; this is what I see all the time, every day," Korrine said.

The kids froze. They realized the super animated and fun speaker who was explaining so many things to them during this talk couldn't even specifically see them. Attention spans of teenagers will wane; however, you could have heard a pin drop in the cafeteria full of teenagers when they realized Korrine only saw them as blurred images. The whole evening, they were on the edge of their seats watching not one but two sisters rolling around in front of them in wheelchairs and sharing stories and information they had never heard before. The teens were both somewhat hypnotized and in an engrossing confused state at times, but they were genuinely interested in understanding the message coming from both Korrine and Alli.

Their entire DABS program had a lasting impact. These teens had first-hand experience to learn seen and unseen disabilities. They learned how much Korrine and Alli were capable of despite those disabilities, too. How many of us get this opportunity? Opening eyes, opening minds, and opening hearts are precisely the missions of Korrine and Alli. They want to raise awareness for those people living with disabilities by changing perceptions the public may have.

Disability impacts all of us! The Centers for Disease Control and Prevention state that 1 in 4 adults in the United States have some type of disability, which is 61 million adults or 26% of the population. It is important to understand that not all disabilities are visible, and not all visible disabilities are as detrimental as they are mistakenly perceived either.

Every person faces different challenges, with or without a visible disability, but those with a disability have tough struggles. Living with a disability is not easy, but it can be done! We can all help by opening our eyes to those around us who are functioning a little less equipped than us. When we see someone with a noticeable disability, it is important not to judge. They'd prefer we get to know them and their disability. Focus on the person by looking them in their eyes. We all appreciate acknowledgement when looked at through the eyes. When someone has very apparent physical disabilities, it is easily forgotten to look them in their eyes instead of what obviously makes them different than us. When we have that communal embrace of the eyes, we can move on to ask sincere questions that are appropriate. Those most acceptable words to use are: "Hello, how are you?" and "Do you mind if I ask you a question about your disability?"

If accompanying young children, instead of telling them "Don't stare," please tell them to say hello. People with disabilities are just like everyone else. They laugh, cry, cough, sneeze, and they even fart! They face the same daily needs, challenges, and problems; however, they may have to approach or handle them differently. They deserve the same respect and acknowledgement as anyone else. Sometimes they don't get the needed respect which leads to discrimination. They are people — not their diagnosis or disability.

Within societies, there exist invisible labels and an ambiguous pecking order of its members that can lead to discrimination. The greater society, in the United States of America, has an elected government acting as the leaders, and thus they create civil rights laws with the purpose of freeing people from certain types of discrimination. Like civil rights for racial minorities and women, the government recognized the need to eradicate discriminatory policies and practices towards those individuals with a disability.

For years, if born with a disability or developed some form of handicap later in life, it was assumed one would fall in the natural progression of consequences imposed by the disability itself. There was nothing in place to help outside of what could independently be done in the situation. The bootstrap mentality of America is a positive force until that bootstrap mentality doesn't reach out to helping the less equipped and more vulnerable neighbor to pick them up also.

Thus, all forms of exclusion existed including the normalization of removing individuals faced with a disability to institutions. Out of sight and out of mind was a perverse and archaic form of thinking. With progress, a movement formed out of advocacy to change these dated and incorrect ways of thinking. In 1973, there was a historic shift with the passage of Section 504 called the 1973 Rehabilitation Act. It was like previous civil rights laws which had prohibited race, ethnic origin, and gender-based discrimination with federal funds. This was finally the first time the exclusion and segregation of people with disabilities was viewed as discrimination in the eyes of the federal government and thus created another class of minority — those with disabilities. The substandard social and economic status of having a disability was finally deemed a result of societal barriers and prejudices and not because of the disability itself. Having a minority class status is imperative in developing and organizing advocacy efforts. Everything takes time, but this was a needed component for people living with disabilities.

The 1973 Rehabilitation Act paved the way for a better civil rights law called the Americans with Disabilities Act (ADA) that was finally enacted in 1990. It prohibits discrimination against people with any form of disability and in any area of public life. Individuals with disabilities have the same rights and opportunities as everyone else per the ADA and per a respectable human soul. There are five main areas the Americans with Disabilities Act covers: employment, public services, public accommodations, and services operated by private entities, telecommunications, and miscellaneous provisions. The weight the ADA carries is enormous, because at times particular groups among people with disabilities are threatened with the removal of protections. With solidarity now found in the minority class of disabilities, they can stand behind the ADA and protect rights for all.

We want to highlight a few aspects the ADA encompasses where we might daily see it in action. If no one has brought these concepts to attention before, let this be a short lesson that will tremendously improve the functionality of those individuals with a disability. It will also make us more socially aware of these often-overlooked social issues of the minority class of disabilities.

If we are already competent on these basic ideas, please advocate and share this information with individuals, particularly with children, who are unaware. The legislative rights compiled in the ADA were battled hard for and were long overdue.

Parking Lots

One prevalent area where we are affected and can see an ADA law is in parking lots. There are specific handicap accessibility parking spots within every public parking place. The rectangular, blue, and white signs, located either printed on the pavement or standing erect on poles, indicate handicapped parking.

Like all laws we obey, handicap parking spots are not an optional thing to abide by. The law of handicapped parking is only for those with a handicapped tag visibly hanging in their car's rear-view mirror or on their license plate. Pressure from limited time constraints in our schedule, or having temporary ill health, are not legitimate forms of disability to warrant the use of these parking spots. We agree the close handicap parking spots are convenient and are tempting to use, but simply put, if we don't have the handicapped parking tag, it is illegal and unethical. We are taking the spot of someone who genuinely needs it. Illegally parking in handicap spots happens all too often.

Public Accessibility

Likewise, in public buildings there are accessibility features to benefit those with an actual handicap and should thus be refrained from use if you are able-bodied.

The large bathroom stalls with arm grip bars are an example of one of those handicapped features. In addition, the large square buttons at waist-height of the entrance to a building are there to press and open the doors. They guarantee the door stays propped open long enough to allow the individual the needed time to maneuver into a facility. When they are in operating order, the automatic doors are a great feature. Ramps in and out of buildings, in addition to elevators and wide door frames, are all examples of improved accessibility.

New buildings built today are required to accommodate all these features, but it is taking time to get all older buildings up to similar code. If our activities were impaired by our physical abilities, we would rely on proper accessibility assistance in public; therefore, we should take notice of our surroundings now and see if public buildings are up to code for someone with a disability.

Service Dogs

Service dogs are another area of disabilities where some of us possibly feel uneducated. In the United States, service dogs are protected under the Americans with Disabilities Act. Therefore, they can accompany their owners everywhere their owners go — including inside restaurants.

Service dogs are purposely trained to be of service to particular people who need their explicit help. The trained dogs should be clearly marked with a blue harness and behold official tags and paperwork. Some trained dogs will also have specific, small tattoos inside their ear to illustrate the exact nature of the animal.

A service dog is highly trained with exemplary skills, and they should not be approached unsolicited. They are working when they are with their owner. Don't be offended, but do not approach to pet a working service dog. If accompanying children, teach and explain to them the dog cannot be distracted. They have a job to do.

If we would like to ask questions, the service dog's owner is exactly who we should strike a conversation and inquire with.

Typically, someone using a service dog would appreciate a candid conversation to share about an important aspect of their lives.

These were very basic introductions to the Americans with Disabilities Act and how it conceivably intersects with our daily life. Whether we feel affected by the ADA or not, a key element to consider is the efficacy of the law and to what degree the law is being fulfilled. It is not uncommon to find non-functioning, push-automatic doors and improperly filled handicapped parking spots. Imagine having a disability and finding these further hurdles to overcome to function.

Those living with a disability desire to blend in with society. They don't want attention, sympathy, or special treatment, and especially not exclusion. They merely need accessibility assistance to balance and blend themselves in with everyone else. The rest of society would do well to understand things like the ADA. Ignorance is not permissible on social issues like civil rights.

In addition to encouraging awareness and education about the Americans with Disabilities Act, we also want to explain some of the predominately used aids by people with disabilities, such as personal mobility devices, adaptive devices, and technological advancement. If it is not something affecting you daily, it is easy to misunderstand what people with a disability use to function daily. Knowledge is power and a genuine tool to bridge understanding with others.

At times, our initial reaction is to jump and help people who are crossing our path with disabilities. This is a great act of being a Christian, but we need to first ask if our help is warranted and preferred. Remember, those living with a disability are just like anyone else and they desire independence just like an able-bodied person. Opening a door for someone is generally appreciated, but physically helping someone through the door is where a little more communication is also appreciated before acting upon the motive. We don't invade personal space unless it is asked.

Personal Mobility Assistive Devices

Walkers, canes, and wheelchairs are all assistive devices used for mobility. Just because someone is in a wheelchair does not mean they are unable to walk, and likewise just because someone is using a cane or walker does not mean they are completely incapable.

The connection between wheelchairs and illness evolved from the use of hospitals using wheelchairs to transport sick people, and it is a misconception we want to correct. People use personal mobility assistance to assist them in blending in with society and they do not intend to stand out in society. They need to move in a more convenient manner with personal mobility assistive devices, including the ease factor for those able-bodied people who are helping them.

Push wheelchairs and automated wheelchairs differ in their mechanism, but they serve the same purpose of moving a person swiftly on wheels. Automated wheelchairs tend to be more cumbersome and bulkier than a simple folding push wheelchair; therefore, accessibility into older buildings is at the forefront of someone using an automated wheelchair. The automated wheelchair runs on its own without someone having to push them, but they must consider if their chair will fit and maneuver into the desired location they are going to. Some buildings simply do not have large enough doors, and many have steps that would halt an automated wheelchair from accessing the buildings.

Alli utilizes an automated wheelchair more often, whereas Korrine utilizes a push wheelchair. This is purely because of their personal situations and the consideration of those people who are helping them. These personal wheelchairs support but do not completely take them everywhere they need to go. A wheelchair is like a bike or car that enables a person to get around with more independence. It is a tool, when used effectively, that makes a big difference.

Likewise, walkers are structured with more support than canes, but they serve the same purpose in aiding a person to walk. In the past, Korrine would refer to her walking canes as her "sticks." They are simply an added aspect of her attire for the day. What is an obvious aspect of her attire by a new onlooker's glances is just an everyday aspect of Korrine. Those who know her well understand this is just part of Korrine, and this is how Korrine would prefer us to naturally view her sticks also.

Adaptive Devices

This book's mission is not to delve into the latest technological advancement advice for disabilities; however, we want to spread knowledge of how much good has come from its onset into the lives of those living with a disability. If we see someone utilizing one of the following items, acknowledge and share with them what parts of it you understand. It could be a wonderful bridge to opening communication and it also shows a sincere and kind interest in them as equal parts of the community. Don't deflect or ignore someone who is using an adaptive device. Acknowledge it.

The Head Pointer

A head pointer is a traditional device, and when paired with technology, is an invaluable tool. It is a very noticeable adaptive device that Alli utilizes daily. Again, a new observer might gawk and stare at her. Alli would want you to understand her head pointer acts as her finger. Alli has spasticity in her arms, so she cannot control her hands to eat, write, or type.

The head pointer uses elastic and Velcro to attach an extending pole to her head. This pole allows her to type on her computer, sew at her sewing machine, paint canvas art pieces, text her friends, and point to the calendar on the wall for her father. If you see someone using a head pointer, do not stare and do not attempt to grab it. Instead, share that you understand it is an adaptive device and that you are glad to see they use it!

Technology

It is a fair statement to assess the impact iPads and iPhones are having for those with a disability as astronomical toward the positive. There are adaptive devices for gaming and for speaking. "Verbally" is a unique app that allows Alli to continue conversation in a more lucid and fluid manner by prompting her with conceivable options for what she would say next. Alli uses her head pointer to press on the smart prompts to communicate a quick reply. The benefits of technology encourage those with disabilities to recognize the endless possible opportunities available for them. Where prior hurdles and obstacles were harder to clear, the paths are now plowed under by the ease and use of technology. They can conquer hurdles quicker because of technology.

Korrine uses a zoom text to magnify physical material she needs to read. Her impaired vision requires apparatuses to help her read. She uses them like her right hand. She also has a secret to help her blend into society. Korrine regularly takes pictures with her phone. Then, she zooms in and can see what the rest of us see readily.

Touch screens allow Alli to use her head pointer in a more effective manner. She is more connected and more capable from the usage of the two, iPad and head pointer, together. In addition, she can now help others with their computer problems from her knowledge and experience with technology.

Disabilities do not determine the role someone can embrace in society, but unfortunately the attitudes of society may render someone with a disability to an ancillary or subsidiary position. Therefore, it is deemed as brave, courageous, and unexpected to see anyone with disabilities ascend to the unforeseen. Even with the Americans with Disabilities Act in place, this is still a perception that needs to change. Education and awareness are the greatest tools in changing perceptions, but it takes time and continuity with repetition of the message. Advocacy doesn't stop if prejudices toward exclusion still exist.

Most people are more comfortable being in a group of individuals who are like them. There is a level of acceptance found within shared experience. We generally feel heard and understood when encircled by peers like ourselves. This is fine. We should be in like groups, but we also need to open our eyes and hearts and broaden the groups we are surrounded by. We might not be like others in a noticeable manner, but we can be like-minded, share a commonality, or share a purpose and goal and still form comfortable bonds. It takes more effort to establish those bonds, but it is worth it.

Finding the commonality that connects us is what we have strived for in writing this book. Inclusion of everyone is important. Alli wants you to understand that you can enjoy being with people different than yourself. When we are not included because of a disability, it hurts. Alli doesn't want anyone to feel the hurt she has, and awareness can prevent that.

We all have different disabilities, struggles, strengths, and weak-nesses. A temporary disability through an athlete's injury will warrant a glimmer of what it feels like to live with inconveniences in function and mobility; however, they generally do not feel the same long-term judgment from onlookers. People with disabilities live more acutely aware of prejudices, struggles, and limitations imposed on them. If we become temporarily disabled, we are receiving a gift to understand what walking in someone else's shoes truly feels like.

We have a choice and the ability to raise awareness and be a form of support to those living in the largest minority group — people with disabilities. Let's not allow another day to pass us by where we deflect and ignore people who are different than us. People living with a disability are just like us. We can make a difference. We can remove barriers confronting people with disabilities by doing the following:

1. Understand and abide by the ADA laws and promote a barrier-free environment.

2. Encourage inclusion and participation of people with disabilities in accessible community activities.

3. Realize children's curiosity around people with disabilities and talk to them about it.

4. Speak up when there is negativity about disabilities.

5. Speak up when there is positivity about disabilities.

6. Accept people with disabilities as individuals who are capable like you, and hire qualified disabled people whenever possible.

Choose to live the golden rule and do unto others as you would have them do to you. The future is unknown, and we don't know how our road and life will intersect with a disability. It probably is not a question of IF but rather WHEN it will happen.

The Road Ahead

My Lord God
I have no idea where I am going.
I do not see the road ahead of me.
I cannot know for certain where it will end.
Nor do I really know myself,
and the fact that I think I am following your will
does not mean that I am actually doing so.
But I believe that the desire to please you
does in fact please you.
And I Hope that I have that desire in all that I am doing.
I hope that I will never do anything apart from that desire.
And I know that if I do this,
You will lead me by the right road,
Though I may know nothing about it.
Therefore I will trust you always,
Though I may seem to be lost
And in the shadow of death.
I will not fear,
for you are ever with me
and you will never leave me to face my perils alone.

Fr. Thomas Merton, OCSO

❓ Reflective Questions

1. Who do you know that uses adaptive devices for accessibility?

2. How can you help someone to gain better accessibility?

🙏 Closing Prayer

God, please help me remember that you created every person I see and that your Son died on the cross for every person I meet. Help me also remember having a disability is not who a person is. They are made in your image, God, just like me. They determine what their disability is to them, not me. God, I ask you to place people in my life that I can help with the gifts you have given me. I want to be positive and patient. I want to glorify you, God, in all that I do. Blessed be your name, God. Amen

CHAPTER THIRTEEN

Able to Love

Not only that, but we even boast our afflictions,
knowing that affliction produces endurance, and
endurance, proven character, and proven character,
hope, and hope does not disappoint, because the
love of God has been poured out into our hearts
through the holy Spirit that has been given to us.

† Romans 5:3-5

As told by Korrine:

One of my first part-time jobs as a high school student was working in a medical office as an administrative assistant. This was for a neurologist who visited irregularly to see patients in the local area as a satellite location to his main office in the city. I only worked there during a summer session while also working as a lifeguard.

This small fragment of my history left a lasting impression on me. It brings things full circle in my life now as a married, mother of four living with MS. Occasionally, something that seems trivial and fleeting in the moment later returns to us in thought as a deluge of reflection later in life. This is the case for me on this story.

One afternoon, a patient left the neurologist's exam room, stormed through the waiting area, and left through the front doors without even stopping by my reception desk to check-out. The patient was crumbling in tears as though her whole world had come crashing down around her. What must have happened in that exam room for her life to change so abruptly? Her husband was visibly upset, consoling her, and practically carrying them both out of the office. To say they were devastated is an understatement.

I was given the lady's chart from the neurologist. In his somber, quiet demeanor, he told me to call and schedule a follow-up MRI at the hospital for the young couple. In the notations that needed dictated over the phone to the hospital, it read multiple sclerosis for the diagnosis of this patient. This traumatic incident for that patient came flooding back to me almost ten years later in the moments Chad and I heard the same diagnosis for me: MULTIPLE SCLEROSIS. Life eerily can foreshadow what is to come. It also prepared me to choose love above all things.

Recently after returning home from an evening filled with multiple basketball games, Chad parked our vehicle and we all started the process of unloading everyone and everything from an entire evening away from home. I had one misstep while getting out of the car and I toppled to the ground. This is not abnormal for me. I have MS. I fall.

In my experienced wit, I immediately responded to my attentive boys peeking around the car doors, "Oh, I'm just checking the air pressure of the tires."

And just as assuredly, Chad came around the corner to concur, "I agree, the tire pressure does seem a little low. I better get on that."

I function to negate any sympathy for my circumstances. My ego has been bruised through years of inadvertently rolling into the wrong public bathrooms from my impaired vision, from missing a step and falling, and from burning myself on a hot pan from the oven; but this hard-earned experience has garnered me the quick-wit and quick heart to help anyone else who has a stumble that results in a bruised ego.

Alli and I suffer from diseases that have no known cures. There is no magic wand to take away our daily ailments. Multiple sclerosis and cerebral palsy do not have a cure. The weight of MS is heavy. The weight of Alli's CP is heavy. Make no mistake about it, we are fully aware. Yet, above all things, we are choosing love.

Morrie Schwartz, in the book *Tuesdays with Morrie* said, "Build your own subculture. I don't mean you disregard every rule of your community. I don't go around naked, for example. I don't run through red lights. The little things, I can obey. But the big things — how we think, what we value — those you must choose yourself. You can't let anyone — or any society — determine those for you." Alli, Mom, and I have built our own sort of subculture within our family, a subculture within a larger circle comprising extended family and friends, and yet another subculture within an even larger circumference of our school, church, and community. These subcultures, like Morrie Schwartz discusses, are an important aspect of being able to maintain hope.

Morrie went on to explain: *"The problem is that we don't believe we are as much alike as we are. Whites and blacks, Catholics and Protestants, men and women. If we saw each other as more alike, we might be very eager to join in one big human family in this world, and to care about that family the way we care about our own . . . We all have the same beginning — birth — and we all have the same end — death. So how different can we be?"* So true. Disabled and able-bodied, we are all more alike than we think.

How different are we really? Morrie Schwartz had reflective time in analyzing life as he battled a horrible disease to his death. Alli and I are walking this life with disabilities in a perpetual manner with chronic pains to manage, but with the same resounding beliefs Morrie Schwartz advised as he neared death. How different are we really?

Our afflictions over the years have produced fortitude. The Holy Spirit has molded us. Allison is an inspirational light to people she meets, but she will quickly remind me of how formidable my luminary light is for the students I help daily as well as for my own sons. This *is* the Holy Spirit of God shining through us if people see His light.

We are fulfilled because we choose love. When we make positive choices with the Holy Spirit, the result is to live in a more peaceful place. Good choices have been clearly displayed in this book, but what about all of us? What is the one thing we know we need to change for the better? Make a choice today to change for the better with God's Word as a guide. Do it to live in a more peaceful state. Don't wait for an epiphany event to motivate change. The big epiphany may never come; or worse, it will come, but the wake-up call won't be enough to shake us.

Hans Urs von Balthasar said, "What you are is God's gift to you. What you make of yourself is your gift to God." Think long and hard about it. This is a very intimate request but take a pause. Spend some serious moments considering and reflecting on the fact that you simply being here on earth is a gift from God. And then, truly what we make of our life is the gift we can return to our maker, our father, God.

Every ounce of our being, from our worst scar and worst behavior to our best achievement and kindest act, combines to make this great gift that is us. Whether we are a gifted athlete with a very able body or a body that can endure long hours of hard labor, whether our body moves imperfectly or doesn't move at all, it is the gifted body we were given. Every physical feature on us, even the things we least covet, are all gifts! No one can take it away from us because it is a God-given gift. It is as simple as that.

Will we receive what we are? Will we readily love the gifts God gave in our body? Then, what we do with this body, this soul, and this time of life is our gift in return to God. What we do with this gift is NOT something to be highlighted on social media for all to see, though. God doesn't need partial aspects of us posted on public display. This is a much more profound gift we can give back to God. It is far bigger and far more personal. It is our heart. We give our heart to God. The Spirit leads our heart to do God's holy will with our life. This will intimately join us with our maker.

God transcends time. For God, there is no time as we know it with physical clocks containing minutes, hours, and days. He can see everything all at once. Everything that ever was or will be is laid out in front of God at the same time. This is further elaborated on in 2 Peter 3:8 *"But do not ignore this one fact, beloved, that with the Lord one day is like a thousand years and a thousand years like one day."* We see the present moment, but God sees everything in a single moment. God's providence is his foresight and foreknowledge, yet God provides us with our own making, complete free-will.

C.S Lewis wrote, "Don't shine so that others can see you. Shine so that through you others can see Him." We are sisters in wheelchairs, and we are on a mission with our families to show it doesn't matter what befalls us in life. What matters is how we choose to move forward. Choose to shine bright, and through our holy resignation to our circumstances, bring others to God, too!

We choose to accept our vulnerabilities with a resilient optimism. We humbled ourselves to receive instruction and along the way we gained communication skills. We lean on family and friends and choose not to harbor any bitterness or resentment in life. Our faith helps us to understand what it means to live in the moment and to seize the day. And a huge ingredient of living for today equates to thinking of others and bringing them to a better place. We can do this with unpolluted hearts because we have true empathy.

I have almost two decades of living with multiple sclerosis and Alli has over four decades of living with cerebral palsy. We are veterans and well-equipped through our experiences to raise awareness. We are raising awareness for those with physical disabilities, but we are also raising awareness for those with abilities to choose to live a better life for themselves, too. Even amidst the most insurmountable struggles, the effort to make good choices will always lead you to a more constructive and peaceful place. This is what has happened for our families.

So, what does the future really look like? I don't wish to not have MS, but I do wish I could wave a magic wand and have my boys put their dirty laundry the right side out into the hamper! But I'll take it any way it comes, because I am grateful they are healthy!

Life moves forward. This might be the biggest take-away from this book that life moves forward. The show goes on. Janice McGrane S.S.J was a disabled sister who wrote in her book *Saints for Healing: Stories of Courage & Hope* that "What people don't see is the sustaining grace with which God has blessed me. Each of us receives the grace to live our own lives, not someone else's."

So, what does the future really look like? — It looks like this song.

"Boxes (Alex Aldi Mix)"

I need a family to drive me crazy
Call me out when I'm low and lazy
It won't be perfect, but we'll be fine
Cause I've got your back, and you've got mine
You got mine

We'll have tiny boxes for memories
Open them up and we'll set them free
There'll be bad days and some hard times
But I'll keep your secrets, if you keep mine

You are the memory that won't ever lapse
When twenty five years have suddenly passed
Wherever you take me, it's clear I will go
Your love's the one love that I need to know
Your love's the one love that I need to know

Take my picture and then you laugh
Cause I hate the way I look in photographs
Keep your memories, but don't live the past
I'm looking forward to the best days we will have

You are the memory that won't ever lapse
When twenty five years have suddenly passed
Wherever you take me, it's clear I will go

ABLE TO LOVE

Your love's the one love that I need to know
You are the sun in the desolate sky
And your life's in these words and it can't be denied
Wherever you take me, it's clear I will go
Your love's the one love that I need to know
Your love's the one love that I need to know

You can cry away all your complicated memories
That keep you up so many nights
But darling save your apologies
Cause I know that you're scared,
But I swear you'll be alright
I swear you're alright
You're alright

When the answers escape us when we start to fade
Remember who loved you and the ones who have stayed
Cause my body will fail, but my soul will go on
So don't you get lonely I'm right where you are

You are the memory that won't ever lapse
When twenty five years have suddenly passed
Wherever you take me, it's clear I will go
Your love's the one love that I need to know
You are the sun in the desolate sky
And your life's in these words and it can't be denied
Wherever you take me, it's clear I will go
Your love's the one love that I need to know
Your love's the one love that I need to know

❓ Reflective Questions

1. Have you been leading your life in a way that you can look at it right now and realize you have many dreams?

2. After reading this book, what is the biggest choice you realize that you never gave yourself a chance to choose a better option?

🙏 Closing Prayer

Thank you, God, for allowing me to learn more about Gail, Alli, Korrine, and their families. I do not want to place this book on a shelf and walk away futile. Rather, God, I want you to light a fire inside me to discern how I can make better choices in my life, choices that you would want me to make. I want to glorify you, God, in all that I do. Blessed be your name, God. Amen

The Lord bless you and keep you!
The Lord let his face shine upon you, and be gracious to you!
The Lord look upon you kindly and give you peace!
Numbers 6:24-26

Afterword from Laura

Missing an opportunity to be Christ to someone else is sad. Recognizing the mistake and taking it to God in prayer is where personal growth can happen. In God's sovereign power, He always provides us another chance to do good in the world.

In September of 2019, a few weeks before Korrine and Alli asked me if I would help them write this book, I missed an opportunity to act on my Christianity relating to a situation with a physically disabled person.

The incident where I failed to act on my faith involved a quick visit to the local Dollar General Store. I crossed paths with a fellow shopper, a lady in an automatic wheelchair, buzzing up and down the short, overflowing aisles. Her legs were tied securely to the base of the wheelchair and her hand operated the lever to move about.

I didn't want to stare at her, at her deformity, at the thing that made her visibly different than me. Isn't that a likely excuse to evade personal interaction? Did I not want to make her uncomfortable or did I not want to make myself feel uncomfortable? I did attempt to smile at her, but I did not allow my eyes to lock hers intently with the empathetic love all humans need. I am a reserved person, but that should not be an acceptable reason for not interacting.

We eventually crossed paths in the same aisle. Seeing her legs positioned in a distorted manner and tied down, I naively assumed she was brought to the store and was most likely being assisted in the store by the person who brought her. I assumed she surely could not have driven there. Her legs did not appear functioning to get in and out of her chair or a car, let alone to drive a car. Again, I am an adult with a heart for others, yet I possessed pure ignorance regarding physical disabilities in this encounter.

Aside from my regret of not showing love with my eyes, my second regret was that I failed to speak up and ask if she would need any assistance with items located on higher shelves. My heart grieved for her situation. Obviously, I was experiencing the knee-jerk reflex feeling of sympathy that we openly discussed in this book as a less than optimal expression to have. Why didn't I speak up and ask if she needed help? As a busy mom, my brain was trying to remember my own grocery store list by memory. Being distracted in my own thoughts is again not a valid reason for failing to interact.

Mainstream media convictions echoed in my ears. I didn't want to offend her by saying the wrong thing. What are you allowed to say to a perfect stranger now? How are you supposed to talk to someone in her situation? Will I make her feel inadequate by assuming she needs help? What does it really look like to be Jesus to her? I can't blame my reluctance to act on my faith in this encounter on my being an introverted and quiet person, just as I can't blame my lack of interaction with this lady in a wheelchair on the social climate of society, either.

I did nothing wrong because I literally did nothing. This is the wrong I am gripped with — the greatest wrong of inaction. Christ's love would have acted from the heart and not from legalities or personalities. I finished shopping for the list of items in my memory bank, checked out, and left the store feeling like I missed a minor — but true — chance to show a little kindness and love. Those feelings that infiltrate the heart and soul are from the Holy Spirit.

As I pulled out of the parking lot, God confirmed this was a missed chance He had presented me. I now saw the same lady in the wheelchair buzzing on the sidewalk of the town's highway to the south of the Dollar Store. She never had that assistant I naively assumed she would have had shopping with her at the store. She was alone.

Lord, I bring this to you today. Help me to know it is ok to act on the impulse of pure love in your name. Oswald Chambers discusses the topic of impulsiveness and discipleship in his devotional book *My Utmost for His Highest*. He says that the Spirit of God gives a sense of restraint to impulsiveness, which is a childlike behavior, and rather discipleship is built entirely on the supernatural grace of God. Sometimes we restrain ourselves to play it safe, when God is calling us to action and discipleship for Him.

I might have missed my chance on this one occasion to help someone in a wheelchair, but it stayed and ruminated on my heart. When Korrine and Alli asked me to help them on this journey to share their stories in a book, God spoke in my heart that this was a chance to grow and bring Him glory. 2 Corinthians 5:15 says *"He indeed died for all, so that those who live might no longer live for themselves but for him who for their sake died and was raised."* Lord, help me to act on your love daily. I pray this book opens hearts to action and discipleship for God. Our usefulness on earth is perfected through our closeness to God. Please draw closer to God through the sacraments and through His Saints. Line your bookshelves with books on the Saints. A book published recently in 2021 is *Pray for Us: 75 Saints Who Sinned, Suffered, and Struggled on Their Way to Holiness* by Meg Hunter-Kilmer and it would be a wonderful place to start after reading this book and feeling Korrine, Alli, and Gail's love.

How can I be God's quiet hands on earth? Finish this statement: Because I love God, I will . . .

Glory and praise to God. Amen.

Laura Seger McAninch
segerl2@hotmail.com

Resource:
Gail & Terry's Marriage Wisdom

This was given to their daughters when Gail & Terry reached 25 years of marriage. They were married in 1975.

1. Faith, Hope, Love — say your prayers

2. Children are important; they liven up your lives. Sit on the lawn with them and do not worry about grass stains.

3. Family and friends are important; do not lose touch.

4. Don't dwell or fight over money.

5. Trust.

6. Truthfulness is important.

7. Talk to each other daily, communicate openly — it is impossible to read each other's minds.

8. Spend quality time together — at least 1-2x per year get time out/away from all others.

9. Never hold a grudge — forget and forgive.

10. Sex is an important part of marriage.

11. Humor is important. Laugh with each other.

12. Sometimes you sacrifice things you love for your partner.

13. Always look to find the positive.

14. Arguments; angry voices may lead you to few choices.

15. Think before you speak, especially when angry.

16. Never let anger built; express it calmly.

17. Let each other do their own thing; don't dominate.

18. Try new things; do not get stuck in the same routines.

19. Surprise each other.

20. Help each other with household/yard chores.

21. Get it, Keep it, Help each other with it — self-esteem and confidence. Build your own & each other.

22. Listen more, talk less.

23. Don't let material items become important.

24. Daily hugs and kisses. Kiss each morning, hug each evening.

25. Take time to listen to those older than you.

Stop sweating the small stuff. Cherish the relationship you have with each other and with those who love you. Let's think about what God HAS blessed us with. Life is too short to let it pass you by. We only have one shot at this and then it's gone! Have a Blessed Day! Love, Mom and Dad

Notes/Bibliography

1. Albom, Mitch. *Tuesdays with Morrie*. New York: Broadway Books, 1997.

2. Baker, Fr. Kenneth S.J. *The Will of God, Finding and fulfilling Your Purpose in Life*. San Francisco, California: Ignatius Press, 2012.

3. Bricker, Jennifer. *Everything is Possible*. Grand Rapids, MI: Baker Books, 2016.

4. Faber, Adele & Elaine Mazlish. *Siblings without Rivalry*. New York: W.W.Norton & Company, Inc., 2012.

5. Hunter-Kilmer, Meg. *Pray for Us: 75 Saints Who Sinned, Suffered, and Struggled on Their Way to Holiness*. Notre Dame: Ave Maria Press, 2021.

6. Lewis, C.S. *Mere Christianity*. HarperCollins, 1952.

7. McGrane, Janice. *Saints for Healing: Stories of Courage*. St. Anthony Messenger Press, 2011.

8. Mongin, Helene. *The Extraordinary Parents of ST. Therese of Lisieux*. Our Sunday Visitor Publishing Division, 2008.

9. Nouwen, Henri J.M. with Philip Roderick. *Beloved*. UK: 2007.

10. Nouwen, Henri J.M. *With Burning Hearts a meditation on the Eucharistic Life*. Maryknoll, New York: Orbis Books, 1994.

11. Repton, Margaret by Sr. Gesulda of the Holy Spirit. *St. Theresa the Little Flower*. Published by the Daughters of St. Paul, 1960.

12. Rev. Pius Franciscus, O.F.M. Cap., *Mother Love Prayer Book for Christian Wives and Mothers with Information about the Confraternity of Christian Mothers*. Pittsburg, PA.: 1986.

13. St. Meinrad Prayer Book. St. Meinrad, Indiana: Abbey Press, 1995.

14. Weaver, Joanna. *Having a Mary Heart in Martha World*. WaterBrook — Penguin Random House, LLC., 2000.

About the Authors

Gail Werne and her daughters Katelyn Willis, Allison Werne, and Korrine Whitehead.

Korrine Whitehead is a loving wife to Chad since the year 2000, a mother to four growing teenage sons, and a teacher by trade. She has lived with multiple sclerosis, MS, since 2004. Her greatest love right now is supporting and cheering her boys on while they play their many sports. Her outlet to clear her mind now, instead of her former hobby of running, is the activity of doing her large family's laundry after their events! Her body has admittedly changed, but her mind and heart are stronger than ever before.

Alli Werne was born with cerebral palsy in 1981. She lives with her parents, Gail and Terry, and her canine for companion and independence dog, Seal. Alli is a very active Special Olympics athlete and she's involved in the Athletic Leadership Program with Special Olympics. Alli enjoys sewing, painting, and gardening in her greenhouse, in addition to sharing her computer skills by helping others with their technological devices.

Gail Werne is a semi-retired registered nurse. She's active with church, Special Olympics, and running her children and grandchildren everywhere they need to be.

Korrine & Alli are happy to give presentations jointly to groups who wish to hear them speak. They currently provide talks to school age children and teenagers as well as sports teams and women's groups in a Christian setting. Their presentations can be catered to your specific group, speaking about faith, hope, and optimism as well as disability awareness, service dog awareness, and overall inspirational talks for athletes. It is a pure joy to share their company and embrace their witness. You will not walk away from hearing them speak uninspired to change. They can be contacted/followed via: twoabledsisters@gmail.com.

Laura Seger McAninch is a proud, cradle Catholic who loves God. She tries to follow God's will in life, which included writing this book with the Werne ladies. Her quiet spirit finds purpose from living in a simple place with God and her family. It is an honor to bring your name to God in holy prayer. Laura can be reached at seger12@hotmail.com.

Made in the USA
Columbia, SC
23 October 2022

69884580R00111